I0436649

HIDDEN

Prepper's Secret Edible Garden

Jill b.

ISBN: 1535134399
ISBN-13: 978-1535134392

CONTENTS

The statements in this book have not been evaluated by the FDA. This book not intended to diagnose, treat, cure or prevent any disease.

CAUTION:

PURCHASE EDIBLE VARIETIES FROM REPUTABLE COMPANIES TO PLANT IN YOUR PREPPER GARDEN. It is important to note that certain species of the plant are edible while others are <u>toxic</u>. In other cases, some plants may be entirely edible while only certain parts of others are edible.

Ensure that you are harvesting the correct portion of the plant, at the correct time and preparing it correctly before consuming. This book for informational and entertainment purposes only. It is not intended as medical advice. Always consult a professional healthcare provider before trying any form of therapy or if you have any questions or concerns about a medical condition. Natural and edible products can be toxic if misused. When suitably used, certain individuals could have adverse reactions. Please be mindful when consuming new foods, especially if you have sensitivities.

1 INTRODUCTION

Need to hide some edible plants in plain sight? This book offers some suggestions.

Unfortunately, most Americans have become so far removed from food sources that many would probably not recognize food in its original form. The plus side to this is that *you* can take advantage of this ignorance.

This book is written in the same vein as the previous books in this SHTF series, "Foraging -- A Beginner's Guide to Wild Edible and Medicinal Plants" and "Medicinal Herb Gardening -- 10 Plants for the Self-Reliant Homestead Prepper" (http://byjillb.com).

Instead of trying to cover a wide range of edible plants that can be disguised as landscaping plants, I have chosen ten plants for these traits: ease of cultivation in most of the Continental US (because who wants to tend to fussy plants when SHTF?), the low risk of the plant being recognized as a food crop, versatility as a food crop and visual appeal.

There are many good books written on edible plants but I can't think of any that have curated plants in this manner. Why only focus on ten plants? Because if you're like me, you're probably not going to plant 500 edible plants in your yard. Ten is a nice round number which hopefully, will help to prevent analysis paralysis.

These plant suggestions may also help preppers and/or homesteaders wish to grow some food in their front yard but need to stay compliant with their Homeowner's Association (HOA) covenants or city ordinances. City ordinances or HOA covenants vary and can change over time. **I do not know any of them so please do your own due diligence before planting any of these plants on your property.**

Of course, in a dire SHTF situation, none of these plants would likely adequately feed someone. These plants should be seen as supplemental food than can provide a more variety to your other food prep.

2 AMARANTH

Amaranth

Native to the Americas, Amaranth has dozens of species which fall under botanical genus name, *Amaranthus*. The name comes from the Greek word "amarantos", which means "unfading flowers" for its long-lasting blooms. Amaranth is also known as "Love-Lies-Bleeding".

Because of the many varieties that exist, Amaranth can be wild or cultivated, bushy or spindly, ranging in heights from 3 to 10 feet. There are weed varieties, showy ornamental varieties, vegetable varieties and grain varieties. The grains can vary in color from green to red to orange to deep yellow. The plant will grow under a variety of conditions and climates and is one of the few plants that will tolerate drought, high heat and humidity. While there are no poisonous varieties, their palatability will vary so I recommend planting varieties bred for their edibility.

For ease, I will refer to it as a grain, although Amaranth is technically a pseudograin. An annual or short-lived perennial, it is an ancient, nutritious crop that can be used as both a leafy vegetable as well as a high-protein grain. It may be used as a forage crop and has even been used to treat toothache and fevers.

Choose the variety that will suit your needs and climate. Most varieties require a long growing season and may not mature completely in climates with a shorter season. There are at least two varieties though, Love-Lies-Bleeding Red Amaranth and Opopeo-Amaranth, that have a shorter maturity time of 60 days.

In more temperate climates, where maximum temperatures do not exceed 90°F, you might want to consider growing Quinoa, which is also part of the Amaranth family, instead. Amaranth is not frost-tolerant while Quinoa resists light frosts, especially if the soil is dry. However, high heat and warm nights will inhibit the fruit from setting. Cultivars like "Cherry Vanilla" and "Brightest Brilliant" have pretty, colorful edible seed as well as edible greens which taste similar to its close relative, Lamb's Quarters.

According to "Alternative Field Crops Manual" by the University of Wisconsin and University of Minnesota Extension Service, Amaranth can produce "over 1000 pounds of grain per acre in the upper Midwest, though a portion of this grain yield may be lost in harvesting." Amaranth's rapid growth, high rate of seed production, reproductive prowess, relative ease of cultivation, high nutritive properties, culinary versatility, visual appeal and the relatively low risk of it being identified as a food crop make it an excellent addition to your secret prepper food garden.

Cultivation

Because Amaranthus is a widely adapted genus, it can be grown in most of the US as long as the growing season is long enough. In regions with a shorter growing season, the Amaranth may not be able to reach complete maturity before killing frosts arrive. In such cases, Amaranth can still be harvested for their greens.

Amaranth is adapted to slightly acidic to slightly basic (pH 6.5 to 7.5) soils. It prefers to grow in full sun and in rich, well-drained loamy soil but will grow in average soil. It will not, however, perform well in heavy clay and/or poorly aerated soils.

It's best to direct sow your seeds but in areas with shorter growing seasons, start them indoors because Amaranth is susceptible to frost. Start your seeds indoors 6-8 weeks before the last frost. For direct sowing, plant the seeds after danger of frost has passed and when the soil has began to warm up (around 65°F).

The planting bed should be weeded before planting. If the soil is dry, water it before planting the seeds. Because the seeds are very small, you will need to have a firm, fine seedbed. Depending on the soil texture and moisture during planting, the seeds should be planted at no deeper than 1/4 inch deep. Cover lightly with soil. Another way to simplify the sowing process and to avoid having to thin seedlings considerably is to mix the seeds with sand before sowing.

Be sure to keep the planting bed weed free, especially in the beginning. Amaranth will tolerate some crowding so thin the seedlings to about 10-12" apart. Continue to discourage weed by mulching. If the soil is moist enough, do not water until the seedlings have reached the 2-3 leaf stage. Growth is slow in the first few weeks but once the Amaranth reaches about a foot tall, it starts to grow quickly, crowding weeds out.

Potential Problems

Amaranth suffers from few major diseases. However, young seedlings may suffer from damping-off in overcrowded conditions or in instances where the soil is high in water content and low in temperature. You can prevent this problem but removing these environmental conditions.

Flea beetles, Amaranth weevils, leafrollers and tarnished plant bugs are all potential insect pests. Flea beetles and adult Amaranth weevils will damage the leaves, while larval amaranth weevils will cause the stems and roots to rot. Tarnished plant bugs affect the Amaranth seed-fill. Use Pyrethrin to kill these pests.

Harvesting

You can harvest the Amaranth leaves at any time, preferably before the plant flowers. The young leaves are milder and more tender while the older leaves are better cooked. They can be prepared in the same manner as you would prepare spinach leaves. The stems are also edible although the older stems need to be peeled, which is not necessarily worth the effort.

Amaranth buds are edible but if you are looking to harvest the grain, let the plant flower. The leaves are can still be eaten but the flavor will change. As its Greek name suggests, Amaranth flowers until the first hard frost. However, unless the growing season is short, the seeds will often be ripe weeks before that.

To see if the seed is ready for harvesting is to rub the flower heads between your hands and see if the seeds fall out easily. You can also test the seeds by gently but firmly shaking the flower heads to see if they fall out. The arrival of birds are also indicative of the seeds being ripe.

Collect the seeds on a clear, dry day. Put a paper bag over the top of the seedheads and carefully tip the plant sideways. Shake gently until the seeds come loose. If you have a lot of seeds to gather, you can tip the seedheads carefully into a dry, clean bucket, rubbing the seedheads between your hands. Separate the chaff from the seeds by placing them on a screen and winnowing them with a fan. In some cases, you may need to use heated air to dry them.

On the other hand, Quinoa seeds are ready to be harvested when the leaves have fallen off. Light frost will often have set by this time. As long as the Quinoa seed is past the green stage before it's hit by frost, it should suffer from little damage. Harvest after a day or two, on a clear, dry day.

Ensure that the seeds are dry before harvesting. If the seeds have been rained on, they can germinate so make sure that they are properly dry before storing. With a gloved hand, strip the seeds off the stalk into a clean, dry container. Clean the Quinoa by placing the seeds on a screen and winnowing with a fan.

You can harvest the seeds as long as you can barely indent the seeds with your thumbnail. However, being able to indent the seed indicates that the seed is not completely dry and will need to be dried thoroughly before storage. To dry the seeds, expose them to an indoor heat source or to the heat of the sun. Stir the seeds occasionally until they are as dry as possible. A good way to for complete dryness is to see if the seeds break when you press your thumbnail into them. Store the dried seeds in a cool, dry place in an air-tight container.

Propagation

Amaranthus will cross with each other so if you want to save pure seeds, make sure that your planting area is free of weeds like lamb's quarters and red-rooted pigweed, which are related to both Amaranth and Quinoa. That said, you will also need to keep Amaranth and Quinoa away from each other by planting only one cultivar at a time, or planting different cultivars as far away from each other as possible.

Food Uses

Amaranth and Quinoa have sustained the Aztecs and Incas respectively. It is believed that before the Spanish conquest, Amaranth provided the Aztecs with up to 80% of their caloric intake.

"Alternative Field Crops Manual" by the University of Wisconsin and University of Minnesota Extension Service notes that Amaranth grain is high in fiber and low in saturated fats. It not only has 12 to 17% protein but is also high in lysine, which is an essential amino acid that most cereal crops are low on. It is also high in Vitamins B and E, zinc and potassium. Amaranth leaves are also a good source of carotene, iron, calcium, protein, vitamin C and trace elements.

Neither Amaranth or Quinoa have hulls that need to be removed. However, Quinoa is covered in saponin, a bitter, soapy substance that makes the seeds unpalatable to wildlife. Quinoa therefore needs to be rinsed thoroughly before use.

Quinoa normally needs to be rinsed with about five changes of clean water before the frothiness is adequately washed off. If you mix Quinoa in small quantities with other flours, the concentration of saponins present might be low enough that it is unnoticable. In this case, you might be able to get away with less or no rinsing before use. I personally prefer to rinse it thoroughly before use. Amaranth does not have saponins and does not need to be washed in the same manner before consumption.

Grain Amaranth is commonly ground into flour which is then used to make flour-based products including breads, pancakes, granolas, cookies and noodles. It may also be popped as you would popcorn and eaten as puffed cereal; or it can be flaked for an oatmeal-like dish. The Peruvians even use Amaranth grain to make a beer. Its leaves are often boiled or fried and served as a dish.

Flour

You can make Amaranth flour by running the prepared grains through a flour mill. If you are a prepper, it would be a good idea to have a mill that has a hand crank option. However, in everyday situations, unless you like to do things the old-fashioned way, I recommend milling flour using electricity. Milling manually is quite painstaking.

Both Amaranth and Quinoa flour can be used as a substitute for wheat flour. However, Amaranth flour tends to make baked goods more dense. While you can substitute up to 25% of the flour in your recipe with Amaranth flour, the palatability declines when you substitute upwards of 15% of the flour.

Quinoa on the other hand produces a moist, tender crumb with a slight sour taste. It can be used as a 50-100% substitute for wheat flour and is best used for breads and cookies, where high-protein flour is needed.

Porridge

You can also turn Amaranth or Quinoa into a porridge. The simplest recipe is to add the grains to water in equal parts and bring to a boil. Cover and reduce it to a simmer until all the water is absorbed. Cooking Amaranth porridge normally takes about 10-12 minutes while Quinoa takes about 12-15 minutes. You may wish to add a higher amount of water for a more porridge-like consistency.

Popped Cereal

Both Amaranth and Quinoa seeds can also be popped in a manner similar to popping corn. To pop the grains, coat a deep saucepan with cooking oil. If you want the popped cereal to keep longer, you can also dry-pop with seeds without any cooking oil.

Heat the pot on medium high heat until it reaches almost smoking point. Add enough seeds to coat the bottom of the pan in a single layer. Keep stirring the seeds until they start to pop. Cover and turn the heat down to medium-low. Agitate the pot over the heat to ensure that as many seeds as possible are heated to the popping stage. If the seeds start to smell too toasty, remove the pot from the heat but continue agitating the pot. As soon as most of the grains are popped, remove them from the pot. Repeat the process if you have more seeds to pop.

Popped Amaranth or Quinoa can be consumed with milk or a non-dairy milk as you would a puffed cereal. While delicious as a cold cereal, avoid the urge to turn your popped grains into rice crispy-like treats. Unlike popped rice, these tend to not retain their crispiness when molded into crispy-snacks. However, they can be mixed into granola after the granola has been baked.

According to bon appetit, popped Amaranth or Quinoa also work well in addition to or as substitute for croutons on top of salads. It can also be stirred into sweet or savory yogurt or sprinkled over roasted vegetables.

Sprouted Amaranth/Quinoa

Sprouting the seeds is a good way to increase the nutritional value of the seeds. In particular, the sprouting process reduces the amount of anti-nutrients like Phytic acid, which is present in the seeds, particularly in Quinoa. These anti-nutrients can bind with other essential minerals that are present in the grains, reducing their bioavailability.

To sprout your seeds, soak, wash and drain repeatedly for a few days. 2/3 cup of seeds will yield about 1 cup of sprouts.

1. Rinse the seeds to remove any plant debris or dust.
2. If you're sprouting Quinoa seeds that have not already been pre-washed, run the seeds under clean, cool water until the water runs clear to remove the saponins. (Sprouted Quinoa has an acquired taste).
3. Transfer the seeds into a clean container or a sprouter, if you have one. A sprouter is not necessary but makes the process more convenient.
4. Mix the seeds in 2-3 times its volume of cool water (60-70°F).
5. Soak for 20-30 minutes (optional step but soaking will speed the sprouting process).

6. There may be nutrients in the soaking water so save it for watering your plants. Drain the soaking water and empty the seeds into your sprouting container or sprouter.
7. The container should be drained **thoroughly**.
8. Rinse with cool water and drain **thoroughly** again.
9. Set your sprouter or container in an undisturbed spot, at room temperature (around 70°F), out of direct sunlight. I like to keep the container covered with a muslin cloth or a coffee filter.
10. Repeat the rinsing and draining process every 8-12 hours.
11. Depending on your climate and personal preference, the sprouts should be ready in about 2 days -- when tiny roots appear.
12. Drain the sprouts as thoroughly as possible -- it should feel dry to the touch before being stored in the fridge in a sealed container or ziplock bag.

While both Quinoa and Amaranth can be sprouted for a slightly longer time, it will turn from being soft-crunchy to being very soft as time goes on. Short sprout-time seeds will last in the fridge for up to two weeks while older sprouts won't keep as well. Taste your sprouts after every rinse to help you to decide on when to arrest the sprouting process.

Sprouted Amaranth and Quinoa can be eaten raw as a salad topping; steamed or boiled as you would rice, or added to stir-fried dishes. You can also turn the sprouted grains into flour by thoroughly air drying them or drying them in an oven before milling. They can also be dry-roasted on a skillet. Once dry and cooled, they can be ground into a flour in the same manner as you would mill the unsprouted seeds.

Vegetable

When harvested young, both Amaranth and Quinoa greens can be used as salad greens. The greens can also be juiced in small amounts with carrots or vegetables. Older greens can be cooked in stir-fries, steamed, or added to casseroles and other stews. Again, the palatability will vary by cultivar and it is a good idea to purchase the seeds based on the traits you are looking for.

Recipes

Amaranth Clusters

Ingredients

1. 1 1/2 cups rolled oats
2. 1/2 cup popped Amaranth
3. 1/2 cup nuts of your choice, toasted and chopped
4. 1 cup dried fruit or a mix of dried fruit of your choice, chopped
5. 1/4 cup honey
6. The whites of 2 large eggs
7. 1/4 tsp salt

Method

1. Preheat oven to 350°F.
2. In a clean large enough bowl, mix all the dry ingredients except the salt.
3. In another bowl, whisk the egg whites with the salt until foamy.
4. Pour the whisked whites over the mixed dry ingredients and mix to combine.
5. Form clusters from the mixture, about an inch in diameter.
6. On a baking sheet lined with parchment paper, arrange the clusters.
7. Flatten the clusters to form thick discs, about 3-inches across.
8. Bake for about 15-18 minutes, or until the clusters are golden brown.

9. Rotate the tray halfway during the baking.
10. Allow the clusters to cool completely before storing them in an airtight container. They should last for up to one week.

-   *Recipe adapted from Martha Stewart*

Sauteed Amaranth Greens

Ingredients

1. About 4 large handfuls of young Amaranth leaves, washed and patted dry
2. About 5 garlic cloves (or to taste), peeled and sliced
3. 1 Tbsp butter or cooking oil
4. Salt to taste
5. 2 Tbsp water

Method

1. Heat the oil in a skillet on medium heat.
2. Add the garlic and stir quickly for a few seconds.
3. Add the Amaranth greens, salt and water and sautee.
4. Cover and allow the greens to sweat for a minute.
5. Uncover and allow it to cook until the greens are wilted.
6. Serve hot.

Amaranth Greens Pancake

Ingredients

1. 1/2 c Amaranth seeds
2. 1 c water or vegetable or meat stock (using stock will be more flavorful)
3. 1 large bunch of Amaranth or chard greens, washed and stemmed
4. 1 c ricotta cheese
5. 2 eggs, beaten
6. 1/2 c milk
7. 5 Tbsp grated Parmesan cheese
8. 1/2 c + 2 Tbsp pastry flour
9. 1 tsp baking powder
10. 1/2 tsp salt + salt to taste
11. 2 Tbsp extra virgin olive oil
12. 1/2 medium onion, finely chopped
13. 2 large garlic cloves, peeled and minced
14. Freshly ground pepper to taste
15. Cooking oil or butter

Method

1. In a large enough saucepan, add the Amaranth seeds, stock and salt and bring it to a boil.
2. Cover and reduce the heat to a simmer for about 30 minutes or until all the liquid is absorbed.
3. Remove the saucepan from the heat and allow it to sit undisturbed for about 15 minutes.
4. In a skillet, heat some cooking oil or butter over medium heat.

5. Add the Amaranth greens and allow it to cook until wilted.
6. Remove from heat.
7. Allow it to cool before squeezing out any excess water.
8. Chop the greens finely.
9. In a skillet, heat some cooking oil or butter over medium heat before adding the onions.
10. Saute until tender.
11. Add the garlic and cook until it becomes fragrant, about 30 seconds.
12. Add the greens and seasonings, mixing the ingredients well.
13. Remove from the heat.
14. In a large bowl, mix the ricotta cheese, Parmesan cheese, eggs and milk together.
15. Sift in the flour, baking powder and salt.
16. Mix well.
17. Fold in the Amaranth seeds, greens and pepper.
18. Heat enough butter or cooking oil to coat the bottom of a griddle or seasoned cast-iron pan over medium-high heat.
19. Fill a 1/4-cup measuring cup part way with batter.
20. Drop the batter on the heated pan.
21. Repeat until the pan is filled in dollops about 2.5-3 inches in diameter.
22. Allow the batter to cook undisturbed until you see bubbles start to form.
23. When they are lightly brown on the underside, flip the pancakes.
24. Cook the pancakes for another 3 minutes, until the underside is lightly brown. The pancakes should be moist but not raw.

25. Remove from heat and serve hot.

\-   *Recipe adapted from the New York Times*

Crispy Amaranth Leaf Balls

Ingredients

1. 3 c packed Amaranth greens, washed, patted dry and chopped
2. 1/2 c chickpea flour
3. 3-4 green chillis, finely chopped
4. 1/2 tsp ginger, ground
5. 1/2 tsp garlic, ground
6. 1 tsp cumin seeds
7. 1/2 tsp red chili powder
8. Salt to taste
9. Water as needed
10. Oil for deep frying

Method

1. In a bowl, mix the Amaranth greens and all the dry ingredients together.
2. Add enough water to make a dough that's firm enough to form small balls.
3. In a deep frying pot, heat the oil until piping hot.
4. Reduce to medium heat and gently drop the prepared balls into the oil.
5. Fry until the balls turn into a uniform golden brown color.
6. Serve hot.

- *Recipe adapted from sailusfood.com*

Boiled Quinoa

1 cup of dry Quinoa yields about 3 cups of cooked Quinoa. You will need to cook Quinoa in the ratio of 1 cup of Quinoa to 2 cups of liquid. You can use water but using vegetable or a meat stock with about 1/4 teaspoon of salt per cup of dry Quinoa, will make the final product more flavorful.

Ingredients

1. 1 cup uncooked Quinoa, rinsed until the water runs clear; drained
2. 2 cups water or broth
3. 1/2 tsp salt, optional
4. Butter or olive oil, optional

Method

1. (Optional step) Heat the oil over medium-high heat in a saucepan. Add the Quinoa and stir it around for about 1 minute to dry and toast the Quinoa.
2. Add liquid and bring to a boil.
3. Cover, reduce to a simmer and cook for 15 minutes.
4. Turn the heat off and let it stand, covered for 5 minutes.
5. Remove from the heat and let it stand, covered, for 5 additional minutes.
6. You should see tiny spirals curling around the Quinoa seeds. Fluff the Quinoa gently with a fork. If there is any liquid on the bottom of the pan or if the Quinoa is a little too crunchy, return to the pan, cover and cook on low heat for another 5 minutes or until all the water has been absorbed.

Quinoa-Stuffed Peppers

Ingredients

1. 1/2 c Quinoa, cooked (refer to previous recipe)
2. 1 c water
3. 1 lb lean ground beef
4. 2 cloves garlic, minced
5. 1 onion, peeled and diced
6. 6 bell peppers, seeded, cored and halved crosswise
7. 1 (8 ounce) canned tomato sauce
8. 1 Tbsp Worcestershire sauce
9. 1 tsp dried oregano
10. Butter or cooking oil (about 1 Tbsp)
11. Salt and ground black pepper to taste
12. 1 Tbsp chilli powder, optional
13. 1/4 c grated Parmesan cheese, optional

Method

1. Preheat the oven to 350°F.
2. In a pan, heat the butter or cooking oil on medium heat.
3. Add the onions and cook until softened.
4. Add the beef and garlic, breaking up the meat as you cook it.
5. Cook until the meat is evenly browned.
6. Remove from heat and mix in the Quinoa, Worchester sauce, tomato sauce and seasonings to the beef.
7. On a baking dish lined with aluminum foil, arrange the pepper halves such that the hollowed sides are facing

upwards. You may wish to slice a bit of the bottoms off the peppers to keep them standing upright.

8. Fill the pepper hollows with your Quinoa mixture.
9. Wrap aluminum foil over the top of the baking tray.
10. Bake for about 30 min.
11. Remove the foil cover and bake for another 30 minutes or so, until the peppers are tender.
12. Remove from the oven and top the peppers with grated Parmesan cheese (optional).

-   *Recipe adapted from Allrecipes.com*

Other Uses

If you have livestock, Amaranth can also be used as a fodder crop. The Amaranth seeds can be used to supplement chicken feed while the leaves can stalks can be used as a fodder supplement for pigs or goats. Consult your livestock vet before adding new foods to your livestocks' diet.

3 AMERICAN LOTUS

American Lotus

Native to parts of North America, American Lotus (*Nelumbo lutea*) is an emergent aquatic plant that often grows in swamps, lakes or in areas that are flood-prone. It is also sometimes called yellow lotus, water-chinquapin or volée.

A perennial aquatic plant, it can become a nuisance because it can cover large area by spreading its rhizomes rapidly in shallow water. It is therefore not a good idea to introduce American Lotus into most fishing ponds. In fact, **it may be considered invasive in some states so please check with your state's Extension Office before planting American Lotus**.

Lotus Seed Pods

Its light yellow flowers bloom from June to September, and resembles an inverted showerhead. They grow to about 8 inches across. Each flower is held on a long, single stalk above water. The circular blue-green leaves usually grow above the water level, on long stems. The leaves can vary in size, growing up to 2 feet wide. The edible seeds are acorn-like and are housed in deep pits, in a seed receptacle that can be up to around 5 inches wide.

Cultivation

American Lotus will grow in Zones 2-10 and is hardy to -50°F, as long as the pond is deep enough to not freeze to the bottom. The plant needs a full sun and prefers still, shallow water with a mud bottom.

The seeds need to be stratified before sprouting. The fastest way to stratify seeds is to either rub through the seed coat with sandpaper until the white endosperm becomes exposed, or to drill a small hole into the seed's outer coating.

Put the seed in about a gallon of warm, unchlorinated and unfluoridated water. Place your container in a warm, sunny location. Ideally, the water should be replaced twice daily but it should at the very least be replaced when the water turns cloudy. Germination should occur at around 2 to 4 weeks.

Next, use a plastic container with no drainage holes and fill it up to 3 inches from the top with a mixture of 2 parts potting soil to 1 part compost. Make a depression deep enough in the soil to set the seedling roots in. Cover the roots with soil, gently pushing it down. Submerge the seed and soil in water to about 1 inch over the soil surface. Place the pot in a sunny location.

Increase the water level as the plant grows. The water level should be kept just under the new leaves. When your pond water reaches at least 60°F, place some stones or pebbles on the top of the soil to help to keep it in place before lowering the pot into the pond. Instead of using pebbles to weigh the seeds down, you can also wrap regular modeling clay (but not PlayDoh) gently around the seed (leaving the shoot uncovered, of course).

Level the plant such that the first leaf lies on the water and the other leaves emerge above the water line. As your plant grows, you may lower the pot, or transplant the Lotus by firmly anchoring the plant into the mud on the pond's bottom. It should be around 6 inches from the water surface. However, in colder climates, plant the Lotus in deeper water for better freezing and frost control.

Do not fertilize the Lotus in its first year because the fertilizer, regardless of quality, will burn its roots. After that, fertilize the Lotus with a good quality water lily fertilizer tab. Lotus will usually only flower after its first year.

Potential Problems

Pests that feed on plant sap like some species of winged aphids may attack Lotus foliage above the water, causing the leaves to wilt, yellow or curl. The undersides of the Lotus' leaves may also harbor spider mites or whiteflies, which cause the leaves to yellow.

Other insects that attack Lotus leaves include leafrollers, water lily beetle larvae and some leafminer species. Fungus gnats and caddisfly larvae on the other hand, may feed on the stems and roots. They may also feed on flower buds. Attacks from these pests may cause the Lotus to discolor or wilt.

Sucking pests can be removed with a strong spray of water. If there are severe infestations of aphids, whiteflies or spider mites, apply diatomaceous earth, rather than insecticides containing oils or detergents, can affect the fine hairs on the Lotus' leaves, killing or harming the plants. Removing floating plant debris will also help to get rid of places that harbor these pests.

Harvesting

The roots can be harvested year-round but is best in fall. Traditionally, Native Americans will dig around the mud with bare feet, when the mud was soft and the water levels were lower. Once you can feel the roots with your feet, reach down and pull them out by breaking them off.

The shoots and young, unopened, rolled leaves can be harvested from late spring to early summer. The leaves are terrible when eaten raw but are palatable after being cooked in about two changes of water. I consider them to be more of a survival food that for everyday fare. Older leaves can be harvested at any time for wrapping or cooking food in.

The flowers can be harvested in late spring to summer, depending on the climate. The seeds can be harvested from their green pods after the flowers lose their petals, usually in summer through to early fall. To harvest the seeds, grab the seed pod and break the stem by bending it backwards. Once broken off the stem, you can split the pod open and remove and collect the seeds.

The seeds, leaves and roots can be dried for later use.

Propagation

Besides propagation by seed, Lotuses can also be propagated by rhizome. In late fall, when the plant has died back, carefully lift the tubers up and store them in a cool, frost-free location. Storing the rhizomes in living sphagnum moss can help to prevent rotting and mildew.

The rhizomes are ready to be planted in late spring when the danger of frost has passed and when they start to break dormancy. When handling the rhizomes, make sure that you do not break off the "eye", which is its growing tip where the leaves (not the roots) will sprout from. Choose rhizomes that have 2-3 eyes because rhizomes with only one eye have a higher tendency to rot or become infected with disease.

To plant, use a pan that you can slowly lower into the pond as the Lotus grows. Plant the rhizomes horizontally or at an angle of around 15-degrees to the soil surface. The eyes should be sticking upwards and protruding from the soil. Do not cover the eye with soil. Placing a large, flat stone on the rhizome will help to keep it weighed down.

Food Uses

American Lotus makes a wonderful prepper food crop because all its parts are edible and can be consumed raw or cooked. This means that the plant, or rather, the different parts, can be harvested almost all year round. While American Lotus can be consumed raw, it's best consumed after it is steeped in water and cooked, which reduces possible bitterness. The cooking process will also kill any pathogens that might have migrated from the water to the plant's raw surface.

Lotus tubers are high in starch (31.2%) and is a source of protein, oil and some vitamins and minerals. In Asia, both the seeds and the roots are the main parts that are harvested for food while in Native Americans tended to prefer to harvest the roots for food. For winter storage, they cut the tubers laterally and then into one-inch pieces before stringing them to dry for later consumption.

Lotus root is sweet and can be eaten raw (although I don't recommend eating it raw if the environment that it grows in is in anyway questionable), stuffed, stir fried or stewed. The young roots are best used in salads while the starchy older roots are better used in soups. Soaking it in water before use will help to reduce any bitterness.

Like an apple, the Lotus root discolors quickly after it is cut. You can prevent discoloration by immersing it in water with some lemon juice or citric acid added to it. You can also rub salt on it to prevent discoloration. Rinse the salt off before use. In my family, Lotus roots were normally sliced and added to pork and peanut soup.

Lotus seeds were one of those treats that I enjoyed as a child (and still do)! The immature seeds can be eaten raw and have a chestnut-like flavor. They can also be boiled in plenty of water for 20 minutes. Drain and salt to taste for a delicious snack. I'm used to eating them boiled and added to desserts or boiled down and made into a sweetened paste. This very rich, thick paste is then used as a filling in pancakes, pastries, mooncakes or *baos* (steamed buns).

When blanched, Lotus shoots can be served in salads. Its flower stems can be eaten raw or cut into small pieces and added to stirfries. Do not use the leaf stems, which is too tough, fibrous and resinous to be palatable. Fresh Lotus flower petals can be used in lieu of lettuce leaves for pretty miniature wraps. They may also be used as a garnish. When dried, the flowers can be used as seasoning.

Some records show that Native Americans used dehulled, mature seeds as a soup thickener. They also roasted and ground the mature seeds into a flour to make flat bread and porridge. The seeds can also be popped, although I have not tried them prepared this way.

Once the sprout, the seeds are too bitter to be eaten. However, you can overcome this bitterness by splitting the seeds apart and removing the sprouts with your fingers before consumption. Note though, that removing the sprouts is a laborious process.

Recipes

Cooked Lotus Seeds

Method

1. Cover about 1 lb of peeled seeds in enough water.
2. Add about 1 tsp of baking soda to the soaking water.
3. Soak for 2 hours or until the seeds become soft.
4. Drain and wash the seeds well.
5. Using your fingers, slit the seeds open and remove the green sprout inside.
6. In about 1/2 gal of boiling water, add the Lotus seeds and about 6 oz of sugar. Rock sugar is recommended.
7. Serve cold or hot with peeled logan fruit.

Lotus Root Chips

Ingredients

1. 1 lotus root, 4-5 inches long, cleaned and peeled
2. 3 c oil (for frying)
3. Sea salt to taste, or your favorite seasoning

Method

1. Slice the Lotus root into discs as thinly as possible.
2. Dry the slices on paper towels to remove any excess moisture. You can sandwich the Lotus discs between layers of paper towels, starting with a paper towel on the bottom.
3. Gently press on the layers to draw as much moisture out as possible.
4. In a frying pan, heat your oil.
5. The oil is hot enough for frying when a slice of root, placed in the oil starts to bubble gently. If the root bubbles rapidly immediately, the oil is too hot and will burn the root slices.
6. Once the oil is at the right temperature, add enough slices to fill the pan without crowding it.
7. As soon as the slices turn golden brown, remove them from the oil using a slotted spoon.
8. Drain the slices on a plate lined with paper towels.
9. While the still hot, add the salt or your favorite seasoning to taste.
10. Serve warm or hot.

Stir-Fried Lotus Roots

This recipe is extremely versatile and many substitutions can be made according to taste and preference.

Ingredients

1. 1 Lotus root section, cleaned, peeled and sliced
2. 1 1/2 c sugar peas or snow peas, pea "strings" removed
3. 1 carrot, peeled and sliced
4. 1/2 lb shrimp, peeled and deveined or 1/2 lb meat, sliced (optional)
5. 3 cloves garlic, peeled and minced
6. 1 inch knob of ginger, peeled and julienned
7. 1/2 Tbsp soy sauce
8. 1/2 Tbsp sesame oil
9. 1 Tbsp Shaoxing/ Chinese wine or dry sherry (optional)
10. Salt to taste
11. 1 Tbsp oil for cooking

Method

1. In a wok or frying pan, heat the cooking oil over medium heat.
2. Add the ginger and garlic and fry, stirring continuously until fragrant.
3. Add the carrots can cook until tender.
4. (Optional) Add the meat and cook until done.
5. Add all the remaining ingredients except the sesame oil.

6. Mix well and cook for about 5 minutes on medium heat, or until the Lotus root and sugar peas are softened but still slightly crisp and not limp.
7. Turn the heat off and drizzle the sesame oil on top.
8. Mix well and serve hot with steamed rice.

Pork, Peanut and Lotus Root Soup

Ingredients

1. 1/2 lb pork spare ribs or chicken bones
2. 1 lotus root segment, peeled and sliced crosswise
3. 1/4 c raw peanuts, shelled
4. 1/2 gal water
5. 8 red dates (optional)
6. 1 Tbsp soy sauce or to taste
7. Salt to taste
8. 1 Tbsp dark soy sauce* (optional)

Method

1. In a large stock pot, bring the water to a boil.
2. Add all the ingredients except the peanuts and lower the heat to a simmer.
3. Cover and allow the pot to simmer for at least an hour and a half.
4. When the soup is thickened down and smells fragrant, add the peanuts and simmer for an additional half hour.
5. Remove from the heat and serve hot.

* Dark soy sauce is thicker than regular soy sauce and is available at Asian grocers or at Amazon.com.

Chicken Steamed in Lotus Leaf

Ingredients

1. 2 lotus leaves, fresh or reconstituted from dried
2. 2 pc chicken breast or 3 chicken thighs, deboned and cubed, or 6 chicken wings
3. 4 shiitake mushrooms, fresh or reconstituted
4. 6 red dates, halved (optional)
5. 2 sprigs green onions, finely sliced

For the chicken marinade:

6. 1 inch ginger knob, peeled and julienned
7. 1 Tbsp oyster sauce*
8. 1 Tbsp soy sauce (may add a little bit more to taste after steamed)
9. 1/2 tsp dark soy sauce*
10. 1/2 tsp Shaoxing wine or dry sherry
11. 1/4 tsp salt
12. 1/4 tsp sesame oil
13. 1/4 tsp sugar
14. 1/8 tsp ground white pepper
15. 2 sprigs spring onions (white portion, slightly crushed and sectioned)

+

16. 1/2 tsp cornstarch
17. 1/2 tsp oil

Method

1. If using fresh leaves, soak for 2-3 hours and parboil before use. If using dried leaves, soak for an hour and rinse before use. Wipe dry.
2. Rinse the dried shiitake mushrooms and reconstitute by soaking them in very hot water. Cover and allow the mushrooms to soak for at least an hour or until rehydrated. Squeeze dry and slice thickly or according to preference.
3. Remove the stones from the dates, halve them and soak in water for 15 minutes.
4. Mix ingredients #6 - #15 and marinade the chicken in the mixture for 1/2 - 1 hour.
5. In a separate bowl, mix the cornstarch and oil.
6. Mix all the ingredients together.
7. Lay the Lotus leaf on a flat surface with the underside facing up. If there are holes or tears, lay another leaf over it. (Wrapping the food against the leaf's topside will tint the food green.)
8. Place your chicken mix in the middle of the Lotus leaf.
9. Fold the leaf sides over to form a parcel and place it in a baking dish.
10. Place in a steamer over high heat for 20 minutes.
11. Serve hot over steamed rice.

* Available at larger grocery stores, Asian grocers or on Amazon.

Other Uses

Lotus leaf tea is sometimes used for medicinal purposes and said to be calming. Dried Lotus petals have been used to make cigarettes by wrapping tobacco leaves in them. Lotus seeds can also serve to feed waterfowl while colonies of Lotus can shelter ducks as well as house pond aquatic life.

4 BAMBOO

Bamboo grove

NOTE: Bamboo can spread very quickly and is considered invasive in some areas. It may even be banned in some regions. Please contact your local County Extension Office before planting Bamboo.

Known as both a "poor man's timber" as well as "a rich man's delicacy", Bamboo is actually a perennial grass from the Poaceae family. Bamboo is one of the fastest-growing, tough, edible and renewable resources we have. It can be used for food, fodder, building, making tools and as fuel. Bamboo is so versatile that entire books can and have been written about this plant.

There are two main kinds of Bamboo: runners and clumpers. However, out of these kinds of Bamboo, there are over 1500 species. Bamboo can be found in a vast range of climates and habitats, from cold mountain ranges of the Himalayas to the hot tropics of India. They grow in regions as different as East Asia, sub-Saharan Africa, North and South America and Australia.

Bamboo can grow to over 98 feet tall and 12 inches in diameter, or it can be as small as only several inches at mature height. Generally though, most Bamboos grow to a height of 15-39 feet, depending on the species. Unlike trees, Bamboo shoots out at its full diameter, without branching, and reaches its full height within a 3-4 month long growing season.

Once it reaches its mature height, it branches from nodes before leafing out. Depending on the species, the culm (large woody stem) usually lives for 5-8 years. At this point, they are ready for harvesting for use in construction.

A BBC article claims that all Bamboo species are edible but with so many species around, I would err on the side of caution. According to "Nutritional Properties of Bamboo Shoots: Potential and Prospects for Utilization as a Health Food" by Nirmala Chongtham, Madho Singh Bisht and Sheena Haorongbam, these are the commercially available, edible species categorized by region:

Australia: *Bambusa oldhamii, Dendrocalamus asper, D. brandisii, D. latiflorus, B. arnhemica, Gigantochloa atter, Phyllostachys pubescens, P. heterocycla* var. *pubescens,*

China: *Bambusa oldhamii, Dendrocalamus asper, D. brandisii, D. latiflorus, Phyllostachys praecox, P. iridescens, P. nuda Phyllostachys makinoi, P. pubescens, P. viridis, Pleioblastus amarus, Thyrsostachys siamensis.*

India: *B. balcooa, B. bambos, B. kingiana, B. nana, B, nutans, B. pallida, B. polymorpha, B. tulda, B. vulgaris* var. *vulgaris, Chimonobambusa hookeriana, Dendrocalamus asper, D. giganteus, D. hamiltonii, D. hookerii, D. longispathus, D. membranaceus, D. sikkimensis, D. strictus, Gigantochloa rostrata, Melocanna baccifera, Phyllostachys bambusoides, Schizostachyum capitatum, Teinostachyum wightii, Thyrsostachys siamensis, T. oliveri, Schizostachyum dullooa.*

Japan: *Bambusa oldhamii, Dendrocalamus asper, Phyllostachys edulis, P. bambusoides, P. pubescens, P. mitis*

Korea: *Phyllostachy pubescens, P. nigra, P. heterocycla*

Puerto Rico: *Bambusa polymorpha, Guadua augustifolia, Dendrocalamus membranaceus, D. asper, Gigantochloa levis, Melocanna baccifera, Sinocalamus oldhami*

Taiwan: *Bambusa edulis, B. multiplex, B. oldhamii, B. pallida, Dendrocalamus asper, D. latiflorus, Phyllostachys makinoi, P. pubescens* and *Thyrsostachys siamensis*

Thailand: *Bambusa edulis, B. oldhamii, B. pallida, Dendrocalamus asper, D. latiflorus, Thyrsostachys siamensis*

United States: *Phyllostachys dulcis, P. edulis, P. bambusoides, P. pubescens, P. nuda, P. viridis*

Note that Bamboo shoots contain the bitter-tasting cyanogenic glycoside, which turns to toxic hydrogen cyanide. Fortunately, the cyanogenic glycoside present is taxiphyllin, which degrades readily in boiling water. Any Bamboo shoots whose bitterness doesn't boil out should not be consumed. Conversely, there are some Bamboo species that are sold for raw-shoot consumption. While not bitter, I would still boil the shoots in water before consumption.

Cultivation

Depending on the species, Bamboo will grow in USDA planting zones of Zone 5-11, with the hardiest species being able to grow in the lower end of the planting zones. Heavy mulching (a foot or more thick) is very important in the colder regions.

Most large Bamboos (*Phyllostachys*) grow best in a sunny location with 5 or more hours of direct sunlight. They generally prefer loamy, slightly acidic soil with ample water and fertilizer. They need to be protected from competitive weeds, especially when they are newly planted or are still not yet established. Young or smaller plants will benefit from some protection from wind and sun, especially in hot climates.

Bamboos will spread (sometimes invasively) by their underground rhizomes. Controlling the spread of clumping-type Bamboos is a little easier than the runner-types. Regardless, annual root pruning will help to keep your Bamboo's spread under control.

To effectively control Bamboo's spread, bamboogarden.com recommends **properly** installing a 60 mil HDPE (high density polyethylene) barrier buried 30 inches deep. Bamboo rhizomes usually grow in the top few inches of soil unless they are growing in very light soils, or unless they encounter an obstruction, which may cause them to turn downwards.

There should be no air pockets or loose soil around the barrier, which may encourage the Bamboo rhizomes to grow under the barrier. It is therefore important to tightly compact the soil next to the barrier. Do not encourage deep rhizome growth by adding soil amendments more than a foot deep.

The ends of the barrier should overlap by 2-3", no more or less. You can then use either stainless steel strips or clamps that are the same length as the trench's depth, to secure the ends together. Make sure the metal strips are not protruding out of the ground.

A cheaper and possibly easier way to control rhizome spread is to surround your Bamboo patch with a shallow trench, 8-10 inches deep. Check the trench in late summer and in fall to see if any rhizomes have tried to cross the trench. Cut any intruders off. You must check on the rhizome spread in either method.

Bamboo can also be planted in containers that drain well. However, the Bamboo will need more care because when contained, they become more sensitive to heat and cold. They are also more prone to being blown over or prone to the rhizomes rotting from becoming waterlogged.

Potted Bamboo will need to be repotted or divided every 2-5 years. Otherwise, they will become overgrown or rootbound, which may lead them to escaping or breaking from their confinement. Planting in containers may stunt your Bamboo's mature size.

To help to prevent your container from overheating in hot climate, plant in a suitable wooden container that drains well.

Locate it in an area with some shade and provide it with plenty of water -- Bamboos planted in containers tend to dry out more quickly. In cold areas, container Bamboos are more susceptible to freezing and need to be protected in winter. Surrounding your planting container with straw or hay bales will help to insulate your Bamboo's roots in winter.

Planting

In mild climates, you can pretty much plant Bamboo anytime of the year. In cold climates though, you'll need to give Bamboo enough time for the Bamboo to establish itself before the freezing temperatures and frost arrive, killing the young plant. Plant your Bamboo at least 6 weeks before the first frost date. If you are planting in colder planting zones, planting in spring (after the last frost date) will give your Bamboo more time to establish itself before the first frost. In hot climates, plant in spring or fall, when the sun is not as scorching.

Bamboo needs good draining soil so if you have heavy soil, amend with organic material before planting. You can also prepare your planting area by mulching it heavily and letting earthworms to do the work. Dig a hole in a prepared bed that is as deep as the root-mass and 1.5-2 times the root-mass' width. Position the Bamboo such that the planting level is the same as the ground level.

The Bamboo roots are very delicate at this stage so be careful not to damage them during planting. Backfill the planting hole with a 1:1 mixture of organic compost and local soil. Make sure not to leave any air pockets around the root.

The Bamboo should be planted in the hole securely enough such that winds will not be able to knock it over.

Add two or more inches of organic mulch material around the Bamboo but avoid fertilizing during initial planting. Water thoroughly (approximately 1 gallon per 5-gallon container) and continue watering 2-5 times per week, with the actual frequency depending on your climate. Allow the Bamboo to dry out between waterings. Bamboo leaves curling inwards is a sign of insufficient watering.

Tall Bamboo varieties (over 15 feet) may need to be staked during their first year of growth until its root-mass is established. Tall Bamboo can also be guyed with rope tied to the same point on the culms, around a third or halfway up the culm. Depending on how windy your location is, you may need to use 3-4 guy lines, each tied to stakes driven about 1-1.5 feet into the ground and at least 6 feet from the Bamboo. Otherwise, supporting them against a fence can also serve a similar purpose.

As the Bamboo grows, avoid the urge to remove fallen leaves from under the plant because the leaves become a good mulch, helping to keep soil soft and moist.

When the plant is established, side-dress with well-composted manure. A 2-inch layer of high-nitrogen fertilizer should be applied around the Bamboo's base in the summer and again in fall or early spring. You may also add fertilizer to areas where you want the Bamboo to spread.

After about 10 years, the culms will start to die off and will need to be removed. Older culms will compete with younger culms for light and nutrients so cut the old culms off at soil level annually. Pruning will improve the health and appearance of your Bamboo.

Potential Problems

Bamboo does not suffer from many diseases by may on occasion be affected by fungal spots, sooty mold, rot and Bamboo Mosaic Virus. Mosaic discolorations on the leaves before the top of the plant dying back are symptoms of Bamboo Mosaic Virus. It is normally transmitted from infected gardening tools and has no cure. With aggressive pruning with using pruners that are sterilized between cuts, you might be able to keep the Bamboo alive.

Fungal spots are round spots that usually appear on older plants. It is mostly a cosmetic problem that often occur in humid climates. It's best to just remove and destroy these older plants to make room for new growth.

Sooty mold is caused by sucking insects like aphids and mealybugs that secrete a sticky substance called honeydew. The honeydew, when infested with sooty mold fungus, causes unsightly black spots, that can be washed off but will recur unless you frequently apply insecticidal soaps or oils as directed on the label.

Rot may also affect the roots and the Bamboo heart and is caused by a fungus. Mushrooms growing on the Bamboo or on the soil around the Bamboo base is usually a symptom of rot. Unfortunately, it cannot be cured and is deadly to the plant. Remove and destroy the entire plant, including the roots to prevent the disease from spreading.

Harvesting

Bamboo will produce shoots when the soil warms up in spring. If you are in the process of cultivating your Bamboo grove, or if your Bamboo is a new planting, harvest only the young shoots that are growing close to the culm and leave the shoots growing further away from the culm to mature. Unless they are growing too closely and will crowd each other, try to let the biggest, best shoots mature for pole-harvesting.

Using a sharp knife, cut fat shoots that are about 6 inches high, at ground level. If you want a heavier shoot and can are willing to apply a little more elbow grease, you can use a narrow spade to cut the shoot where it attaches to the rhizome, below the ground surface.

The shoots tend to stay fresh longer if you harvest them with the base intact. If the shoots are tough, just leave them to rot. Save the tender shoots for consumption. Once harvested, keep the shoots away from sun exposure because that tends to make them bitter. Wash them with cool, clean water as soon as possible and keep them cool.

Choose 3-5 year old Bamboo to harvest for canes or poles. Canes that are at least 2 inches in diameter with the lowest branches that are 12 or more feet above ground are best for these purposes. Harvest poles in summer, after you've harvested the shoots, so that you create room and sunlight for the new shoots to grow into. You may also choose to harvest in late winter, before shooting starts, and when the insects are inactive. This process will also help to stimulate the Bamboo to produce more shoots the following spring.

Leave behind canes that are better than those harvested and harvest enough such that all the remaining branches can receive light while the grove floor remains shaded. As the grove matures, try to harvest it such that there is an even distribution of canes from each year.

To harvest, depending on the number and culm-size, use a chain saw or pruning saw to cut your poles close to the ground. Cut the poles from below the branches, which will usually yield a smooth, round final product.

The poles should be supported and stored in a way that they do not develop bends. However, bent poles can be straightened by by heating the bend and torquing it straight on posts. The branched tops can be used for fodder or shredded to become mulch for the grove.

Propagation

To propagate Bamboo by division, dig up and divide existing Bamboo clumps in early spring, before the plant starts actively growing. Avoid digging and dividing in the heat of summer or the cold of winter, because viability will decrease.

Using a spade, dig around the outside of the clump. Then, gently lift the clump from the soil with a spading fork. If the clump is big, you may need another person to help with the process.

Next, use a sharp pruning saw to divide the clump into several pieces, each consisting of at least 3 culms that have some root and foliage intact. Discard pieces that lack roots and culms. Trim off most but not all of the foliage if a lot of root was lost in the digging process.

Fill clean, 1-gallon planting containers about halfway with fast-draining potting soil that is high in organic matter. Position a division in each container and adjust the soil level such that the root-ball sits just above the surface. Gently, but firmly compress the soil but be careful not to damage the roots. Top dress with potting soil about 1 inch below the pot's rim.

Water the divisions until the water runs out of the drain holes and again whenever the soil feels dry to the touch. Locate the plants in partial shade, out of direct sunlight until new growth emerges. The divisions can be transplanted to their outdoor location before they outgrow their container.

Alternatively, you can propagate Bamboo from cuttings. To do this, prepare your planting container before taking the cuttings. Make uniform holes a little larger than the Bamboo's diameter, in the potting soil-filled planting tray. To prevent contaminating your rooting hormone, put about 2 tablespoons of the hormone aside in a separate container.

Choose existing healthy plants to take cuttings from. Cut off about a 10-inch section of the Bamboo at a 45-degree angle. The section should have at least two nodes, which is the hard growth-ring that separates the canes into sections; and two internodes, which are the spaces between the nodes.

Dip the top edge of the Bamboo cutting into soft wax and make sure that the center hole of the cutting is exposed. Waxing will help to prevent the Bamboo from drying out during the rooting process. Dip the bottom-end of the cutting into the rooting compound and shake the excess powder off.

Next, stick the end with the rooting-hormone into the hole that you made in the growing medium. Tamp the soil in place to remove all the air pockets from around the cuttings because the air pockets will encourage bacteria to breed. Pour water through the top hole of the Bamboo until the hole is filled with water.

You can also plant the Bamboo cutting horizontally by placing a notch in the internode and exposing the hollow center of the Bamboo. Dip the cutting into the rooting hormone and bury each end in the growing medium, ensuring that the notch you made is facing up and is exposed. Water through the notch into the hollow center.

Mist the soil with water until it is damp but not wet. Then, cover the cutting with clear plastic and place it in a bright location but is out of direct sunlight. Remove the plastic daily for about an hour to allow the cutting to ventilate. This is also a good time to water the center hole whenever it dries out. New growth indicates root development. Once there is a healthy root system, you can transplant the Bamboo to its permanent location.

Food Uses

As a side note, Bamboo seed grain produced from flowering is edible and can be boiled like rice and made into cakes. However, this nugget of information isn't very useful because Bamboo flowers only once every 7-120 years, depending on the species.

Bamboo's edible prize lies in its shoots, which should be harvested before they emerge from the ground. The shooting season rarely lasts more than 2 months. High in fiber and potassium, Bamboo shoots have a distinctive but mildly sweet taste.

The cooler the climate that the Bamboo shoots grow in, the better-tasting. Fresh shoots are hard to come by in North America and are quite different from their odd-smelling canned counterpart.

Boiled Bamboo shoots can be added to a wide range of dishes including, but not limited to, soups, curries, salads, pickles, fried rice, spring rolls, stews, stir-fries and appetizers.

To prepare your shoots, wash the loose dirt from your harvest. Peel the thick, outer sheaths away and cut the tip off. Make vertical, shallow cuts into the sheet-like sheath covering. Bring a stockpot of salted water (about 1/2 tsp salt per cup of water) to a rolling boil before adding your shoots.

Boil for 90 minutes before removing the shoots from the heat and allowing them to sit for about 2 hours. Once cooled, remove the sheath carefully. The Bamboo shoots are now ready to be prepared for consumption, or they can be kept in water, in the fridge for a week as long as you change the water daily.

Recipes

Scalloped Bamboo Shoots

Ingredients

1. 3 c Bamboo shoots, parboiled and sliced
2. 4 Tbsp butter
3. 4 Tbsp flour
4. 1 tsp salt or to taste
5. 4 Tbsp grated cheese
6. Paprika to taste

Method

1. Preheat the oven at 350°F.
2. In a greased shallow baking dish, arrange the cooked Bamboo slices.
3. In a saucepan, melt the butter over medium-low heat and stir the flour in.
4. Whisk in the milk and allow it to thicken over the heat.
5. Stir the cheese in and salt to taste.
6. Pour the sauce over the Bamboo slices.
7. Bake for 30 minutes or until lightly browned on top.
8. Serve hot with some paprika sprinkled on top.

- *Recipe by Mount Vernon Northwestern Washington Research and Extension Center*

Pickled Bamboo Shoots

This is a variable recipe. The amount of pickling solution should be enough to just cover the Bamboo shoots when the shoots are packed in a jar, plus a little more. To figure the amount you need, pack the shoots in the pickle jar before filling it with water. Pour the water into a measuring cup. This amount plus a little more is the amount of pickling solution you'll need.

Ingredients

1. Blanched Bamboo shoots, sliced
2. 1 part seasoned rice vinegar or make your own (recipe to to follow in the method section)
3. 1 part water
4. Fresh garlic, peeled and sliced, to taste
5. Freshly ground black or white peppercorns, to taste
6. Hot chili pepper or red pepper flakes, optional or to taste

Method

1. (Optional) To make your own seasoned vinegar, dissolve 1/2 cup of sugar and 1 heaping teaspoon of salt to 1 cup vinegar.
2. In a non-reactive sauce pan, add the Bamboo shoots and cover with the optional spices, vinegar and water. Add more mixture if the liquid doesn't adequately cover the shoots.
3. Bring the mixture to a boil before reducing the heat to a simmer.

4. Depending on the size of the shoots, simmer for 10-15 minutes.
5. Transfer the shoots into clean jars and carefully spoon the pickling solution to cover the shoots.
6. The pickled Bamboo can be consumed immediately or will keep in the fridge for a couple of months.

- *Recipe by extraslaw.com*

Stewed Lotus, Bamboo Shoots and Pork

Ingredients

1. 1-2 c Bamboo shoots, parboiled and julienned
2. 1 lb Lotus root, cleaned, peeled and sliced into discs
3. Pork belly, cubed
4. 2 sprigs of green onions, chopped
5. 1 one-inch piece of ginger, peeled and sliced
6. 1/2 tsp sugar or honey or to taste
7. 1/2 tsp salt or to taste
8. 1/2 Tbsp soy sauce
9. 3 Tbsp cooking oil
10. Water, enough to almost cover all the ingredients

Method

1. In a pot, bring the water to a boil.
2. Add the pork and boil for about a minute.
3. Remove the pork, drain and set aside.
4. In a wok or large frying pan, heat the oil over medium heat.
5. Add the ginger and green onion and fry until fragrant but not browned.
6. Add and saute the pork belly until lightly browned.
7. Add the Bamboo shoots, Lotus roots, salt and sugar.
8. Stir and mix well.
9. Transfer the ingredients into a large enough stewing pot.
10. In the stewing pot, add enough water to almost cover the ingredients.
11. Add the soy sauce.

12. Cover and bring to a boil over high heat.
13. Reduce the heat to low and simmer for 1.5 hours, until the pork belly is tender.
14. Serve hot with steamed rice.

Other Uses

Bamboo has multitudes of uses. Depending on the species, it can be used to make mats, furniture, tools, fishing poles and even rafts, fencing, rain gutters, utensils, weapons (like spears and blowguns), shelter and bridges.

Many species also store water in their hollow joints. Harvest the water by boring a hole in a Bamboo section to drain the water. Bamboo sections can also be cut and plugged with a wooden plug to make a make-shift water bottle.

When dried and split, Bamboo can be used as kindling for fires. Bamboo leaves can be used as fodder. Medicinally, Bamboo leaves have been used in Traditional Chinese Medicine used to prevent phlegm. Bamboo has also been used for epilepsy, fainting and a variety of age-related mental disorders.

5 CAMASSIA

Camassia

Also known as camassia quamash, camas, small camas, common camas, common camash and quamash, Camassia is native to the northwestern part of the US as well as the southern parts of Canada.

Grown as an ornamental plant, the average person will be hard pressed to recognize that this attractive, perennial plant was actually a food source for many tribes in the Northwest, such as the Cree and Blackfoot tribes.

Like Jerusalem Artichokes, Camassia bulbs are high in inulin, which is an indigestible carbohydrate, that can be converted to digestible fructose through cooking. Its high sugar content (about 30% of the dry weight of the bulbs), gives it a high food value. However, Camassia can produce a lot of flatulence if consumed raw or partially cooked.

Camassia roots were traditionally roasted and eaten as a vegetable, or boiled to produce a sweet, molasses-like treat.

Camassia belongs to the *Camassia* genus and grows from a single, starchy bulb about 1-2 inches across. It normally grows around 1-3 feet tall and produces a number of basal, grass-like leaves with 5-20 pale to deep-blue star-shaped, hermaphrodite flowers. The flowers have 6 tepals and bright-yellow stamens which grow from a tall scape, blooming from May to July. Though the bulbs may look similar, **they should not be confused with the toxic, white-flowered meadow death-camas**.

Cultivation

Camassia grows in Zones 3-9 in sunny, moist but not wet, well-draining, slightly acidic to slightly basic (pH 5.1-7.8) soil. It will also tolerate partial shade if planted in slightly drier soils. If planting in clay soil, amend the bed before planting by adding enough organic material, like fully composted manure, compost and/or peat moss; to raise the bed 2-3" above the ground level. This will help to improve the drainage.

Plant the bulbs in fall. They should be planted about 4" deep and 8-10" apart with the pointy end facing upwards. Water them well after planting, and when the plant is growing or blooming. Provide about an inch of water per week; watering more in hot, dry climates and less in rainy climates. Some foliage or roots may form in the fall.

The buds will appear in late spring and start to flower in early summer. Flowering season is when weeding is traditionally carried out. As the summer winds down, allow the plant to prepare for dormancy by letting the plant yellow and die back before removing the dead foliage. The leaves are ready to be removed if they pull away from the bulb. If they show resistance to your careful pull, the leaves are not ready to be removed. In colder climates, you may wish to mulch the plants in fall.

Potential Problems

Camassia is quite trouble-free, being resistant to diseases and pests. From time to time, they may suffer from aphid attacks, bulb rot or blight. Blight can be prevented by increasing the plant spacing to improve air circulation.

Destroy any plants or parts infected by bulb rot. You can help to prevent the rot from occurring by improving drainage and air circulation by increasing the plant spacing. Wash away aphids with a strong sprays of water.

Harvesting

The bulbs can be harvested at any time of the year, but if you want to propagate the plants, it's best to harvest the bulbs in early summer, when the seeds are ripe (black). Mid-June is also a good time to harvest because it's just before the ground becomes too hard to dig.

If the ground is already too hard, wait until the day after a good rain, or wet the area down with water and allow the ground to soak overnight. This process will help to loosen the soil. Use a digging stick or garden trowel to unearth the bulbs.

Save only the bulbs that are bigger than the top digit of your thumb and replant the rest. Leave some of the largest flowering plants intact at every few feet to allow the flowers to reseed on their own naturally.

Propagation

Camassia can be propagated from both bulb and seed. The bulbs may be dug up and divided in fall, after the leaves have withered. However, in nature, it mainly propagates from seeds. That said, plants grown from seeds may not flower until 2-5 years after planting.

Collect the seed when they are ripe and have turned black. They will need to be cold-stratified for 42-100 days at 34–41ºF. You can do so by placing the seeds in a plastic bag and storing it in the fridge for that period, or you can sow them in 6-inch deep trays or pots and let them overwinter to break dormancy naturally.

Sow the stratified seeds in individual pots, in moist soil, covering them about a 1/4 inch of compost. The seedlings will germinate best in a cool, bright location outdoors. Transplant the seedlings in spring, to a weeded, well-draining bed amended with compost. Mulch with 1-2" of organic mulch to help to keep the weeds at bay. Water well during the growing period in spring.

Food Uses

The Camassia bulb is the part that is consumed. To prepare it, break off and discard the basal root crown. Peel off the dirty, outer skin but leave the inner skin layers intact. Rinse the dirt from the bulbs with clean water.

According to David Douglas, a famous early botanical explorer in the Pacific Northwest, Native American tribes adopted a slow-cooking process for Camassia bulbs. A pit was lined with stones and a large fire was lit to heat them. Then, the fire was extinguished and wet vegetation was placed on top of the hot rocks. Up to 100 lbs of bulbs were then piled into the pit and covered before another fire was lit atop of the pile. The bulbs would be baked for up to two days in this manner.

Since the traditional method of baking the bulbs is not practical for most people, a modern-day alternative for small-scale preparation would be to steam the bulbs in a slow cooker. To slow-cook the bulbs, place an expandable vegetable steamer in a slow cooker filled with water up to a level just below where the steamer sits.

Place the cleaned bulbs in the steamer and cook, covered at medium to high temperature for 36 hours. Check the water level every 3 hours or so and replenish as needed. The bulbs should brown and caramelize after 12-24 hours, much like an onion would. Cook until the Camassia turns very dark brown and smells like molasses. People have also reported success by cooking the bulbs with a pressure cooker at 10 pounds for about 8 hours

Remember that Camassia's indigestible inulins have to be broken down by completely cooking the bulbs. Camassia that is not browned will probably not be sweet and give you a lot of gas or indigestion when consumed.

Once cooked, squish the bulbs flat and dehydrate them on very low heat in an oven or dehydrator until fully dried. To preserve the bulbs as long as possible, seal the dried bulbs in a plastic bag and freeze them until you're ready to use them. When ground into a powder, the cooked, dried bulbs can be used as a thickener in soups or stews. It can also be to make a bread-like cake or boiled in water into a porridge or gruel.

Recipes

Sauteed Camassia

Ingredients

1. 1/2 lb (approx 12) Camassia bulbs, peeled and cleaned
2. 1 Tbsp butter
3. 1 Tbsp lemon juice or white wine vinegar
4. Salt or seasoned salt, to taste

Method

1. In a lidded, oven-proof pan, arrange the Camassia bulbs in a single layer.
2. Add water up to about 1/4 inch deep.
3. Cover and bake bulbs at 220-230°F for 12 hours, checking them after about 8 hours.
4. The bulbs should reach a pale to full golden color.
5. Remove the bulbs from the oven and allow them to cool, before slicing the bulbs into rings.
6. Sprinkle salt on the slices.
7. In a frying pan, heat the butter over medium heat.
8. Add the the sliced bulbs and saute.
9. The bulbs will become sticky and caramelize quickly so stir continuously until they are brown.
10. Remove from heat, toss with the lemon juice and season to taste.
11. Serve immediately.

- *Recipe by honest-food.net*

Other Uses

Medicinally, a root decoction has been use to help to induce labor while a leaf infusion has been used to expel the placenta and to treat vaginal bleeding after birth.

6 DAYLILY

Daylily

This showy, low maintenance and very edible plant makes Daylily an excellent choice for the prepper's hidden edible garden. Native to Eurasia, in particular to the East Asian countries of China, Japan and Korea, Daylilies belong to the Asphodelaceae family and have long been bred for their attractive flowers.

Less known, is that Daylilies have also been used as a food in Asia for hundreds, if not thousands of years. Note though that because of their popularity, Daylilies have been hybridized to produce tens of thousands of different cultivars.

As such, **it is important to note that most cultivars are not edible. Some, like the similar-looking Tiger Lily, are downright toxic. Only the original Daylily, *Hemerocallis fulva*, is entirely edible.** There might be other cultivars that are entirely edible, but the orange, **unspotted** *Hemerocallis* *fulva* (*Hemerocallis* basically means "beauty for a day"), sometimes also known as Orange Daylily or Tawny Daylily, is the variety to consider including in your hidden prepper edible garden.

Daylilies grow to about 3 feet in height and have long, linear, grass-like leaves that fan out in opposite directions from the plant base. The upward-pointing flowers are orange, with three petals and three sepals with a slightly contrasting cream/yellow midrib color. The centermost part of the flower is yellow. Its potato-looking tubers are small and bulbous are also edible.

Cultivation

Daylilies will grow in Zones 3-9 and will grow just fine in neglected areas or in areas that are difficult to tend to. This also means that this variety can be weedy and tends to take over a planting bed.

Unlike most other cultivars, it can regenerate from rhizome fragments left in the ground. These Daylilies spread by rhizome so if you want to keep their spread in check, you'll need to plant them in an area where you can stop the rhizome spread. **Check with your Extension office before planting your Daylilies to make sure that it is not an invasive species in your area.**

These original Daylilies are not fussy at all and will grow in a range of soils from sandy to loamy to heavy clay. It will also grow in dry to moist soil as well as in a range of soil acidities, from basic to acidic soils. Tolerant of poor soil, summer heat and humidity, these plants will grow in full sun (at least 6 hours of sun per day) or partial shade.

In warmer southern climates, you can plant in spring or fall, when the temperatures are cooler. In cooler northern climates, they can be planted at anytime between spring and fall, with spring being the best time to plant.

Before planting, amend the soil with compost. Plant your plants or rhizomes 12-18 inches apart and about 1 inch below the soil surface. Water well after planting and mulch with an organic mulch like straw to help to keep the weeds down and to help to retain moisture.

In northern regions, mulch newly planted Daylilies in late fall to protect them. Remove and destroy any diseased foliage in fall. Otherwise, remove dead foliage in spring. Once established after the first year, Daylilies are tough and resilient, often pushing out other plants in their bed.

Potential Problems

Daylilies suffer from few pests. However, they may suffer from rust, which look like red, rusty spots on the plant. To prevent the disease, remove any diseased foliage, keep the plants from overcrowding and allow good air circulation between each plant. Water only when there is insufficient rainfall, and avoid watering from above. Instead, water from below using irrigation hose if possible.

Harvesting

Harvest the shoots in early spring when they are less than 8 inches tall. At this point of its growth, the emerging shoots are entirely tender. Slice the shoots off just above the soil level. More shoots will re-emerge.

Once the plant is established, the edible tubers that resemble miniature fingerling potatoes, should be harvested between late fall and early spring. They are inedible once they become old and brown.

Cut and collect most but not all the young, white tubers, replanting the remaining tubers for subsequent-year harvests. It is too late to harvest tubers for consumption by the time the flower stalks emerge.

In late spring to early summer, the flower buds can be harvested before they open. While both the buds and blooms are edible, the buds are more tasty than the blooms. As their name suggest, Daylilies blooms last a day while the blooming period usually lasts a month. They normally bloom in April or May in the South and in June or July in cooler climates.

Propagation

Daylilies rarely propagate from seed. Rather, they propagate from their root system. After 3-5 years, the plants will start to clump and become too crowded. This would be a good time to divide and replant the clumps. In northern climates, it's best to divide the Daylilies in early spring or in late summer, after they have bloomed.

Before dividing, remove the mulch, weeds and other debris from the area surrounding the Daylily clumps that are to be divided. Using a shovel, dig a circle about 6-12 inches from the plant base, to a depth of 6-8 inches. Next, push the shovel horizontally under and across the root ball to lift it out.

Brush as much dirt from the root ball as possible and place the dug-up plant on a tarp in the shade. Using a clean, sharp knife, cut out sections that contain 2-3 leaf stems and healthy roots. Using a clean pair of pruning shears, cut the foliage down to about 5-6 inches tall. Cut away damaged or rotted roots.

Plant each division in its own hole, spacing the planting holes about 18-24 inches apart. The hole should be twice as wide as the plant's root ball and an inch deeper. Mound a little bit of soil in the middle of the hole and center the root ball in it, spreading the roots over the mound.

Fill the hole with soil, tamping it down gently after adding every 2-3 inches. Do not, however, compact the soil around the roots. Continue covering with soil until the hole is completely filled to the ground level. Water deeply after planting, then water once a week until new growth sprouts. The soil should be moist but not soggy.

Food Uses

Note that while the Daylily's young green leaves, flower buds, flowers (remove the green flower base) and young tubers are edible either raw or cooked, consuming the raw foliage may cause diarrhea, nausea or vomiting in some people.

The problem doesn't seem to persist if the parts are cooked before consumption. Regardless, always exercise caution when consuming new foods, especially if you have food sensitivities. Old tubers should be cooked. Avoid mature leaves and shoots, which become tough, unpalatable and hard to digest. The stalks are fibrous, stringy and bland -- not really worth eating except in survival situations.

The young leaves and shoots are asparagus-like in taste and can be added to stir fries. The fresh flowers or young shoots (under 8 inches tall) can be chopped and added raw in small amounts to salads or sandwiches.

They can also be cooked in any way for about 10-15 minutes and used in any dish where an onion-string bean flavor would work. The larger, unopened flower buds are also reminiscent of green beans and can be used as a green bean substitute. They can also be sauteed with butter, garlic and seasoning for a quick dish.

The fresh flowers can be used raw to make stuffed hor d'oeuvres. They can also be added to soups or battered and fried, much like you would squash blossoms. Wilted, the flowers, like okra or purslane, may be dried and used to thicken soups. However, I have not tried using them as a thickener. The dried flowers are also used in some Chinese soups such as hot-and-sour soup.

Use only the smaller, firm tubers. However, they are labor-intensive to scrub clean and because I'm lazy, I won't bother with them unless there was little else to eat. While they are described as a potato-substitute, Daylily tubers are more like turnip or jicama. Sliced, they can be added to soups or stews, or sauteed in butter and seasonings and served as a side dish.

Recipes

Daylily Fritters

Ingredients

1. 1-2 lbs fresh Daylily buds
2. 1 c unbleached white flour
3. 1 Tbsp baking powder
4. 1/2 tsp rice flour (optional but will give the fritters more crunch)
5. 1/2 tsp sea salt
6. 1 c ice cold soda water
7. Oil for frying

Method

1. In a large enough mixing bowl, mix the flour, baking powder, rice flour and salt until evenly mixed.
2. Add the ice-cold soda water and whisk gently without over-mixing. Leaving a few lumps is preferable to over-mixing.
3. In a saucepan, add the frying oil such that it is a little more than an inch deep and heat it over medium heat.
4. The oil is hot enough when a drop of batter immediately bubbles when added to the oil. If it browns or starts to burn too quickly, the oil is too hot.
5. Quickly dip the Daylily buds in the batter. You can dip them by holding the green stem, leaving the stem unbattered. They'll be delicious after they've been fried.

6. Carefully add the battered buds in the hot oil without overcrowding the pan.
7. Flip the buds when the bottom side turns golden-brown, around 1 minute.
8. Fry for another minute or until golden brown.
9. Remove the fritters from the oil. Drain them on a plate lined with paper towels to absorb the excess oil.
10. Sprinkle salt on the fritters (optional) and serve hot by themselves or with your choice of dipping sauce.

- *Recipe adapted from Aube Giroux*

Daylily-Shoots Casserole

Ingredients

1. 2 c fresh Daylily shoots, chopped
2. 4 hard-boiled eggs, peeled and chopped
3. 4 oz Cheddar cheese, cubed
4. 4 Tbsp butter
5. 4 Tbsp all-purpose flour
6. ~1 c milk
7. 1/2 tsp Worchester sauce
8. 1/4 tsp Cayenne powder
9. 1/2 c seasoned bread crumbs
10. Salt and pepper to taste

Method

1. Preheat the oven to 350°F.
2. Grease a medium-sized casserole dish.
3. Layer the Daylily shoots, eggs and cheese sauce.
4. Repeat the layering until all the ingredients are used.
5. In a heavy saucepan, melt the butter over medium heat.
6. Add the flour, salt and pepper, stirring quickly until blended evenly.
7. Stir in the flour, salt, and pepper; blend thoroughly.
8. Slowly add the milk, stirring constantly until the sauce is smooth and thickened. Add more milk or water if the sauce is too thick.
9. Mix in the Worchester sauce and Cayenne powder.
10. Remove the pan from the heat.

11. Top the casserole with the cheese sauce before sprinkling the bread crumbs on top.
12. Bake for 20 minutes or until lightly browned.
13. If the casserole is bubbly but not browning, you may broil it on low for a few minutes until the top is lightly browned.
14. Serve hot.

Stir-fried Daylily Buds

Ingredients

1. 2-3 c Daylily buds
2. 1 small can of water chestnuts or 1 c fresh water chestnuts, peeled and sliced into rounds or, 1 c Daylily tubers, peeled and sliced into rounds
3. 1 one-inch piece ginger root, peeled and julienned
4. 1 Tbsp soy sauce
5. 1 Tbsp corn or tapioca starch
6. 1 tsp sugar
7. 1/2 tsp fish sauce (optional)
8. 3 Tbsp water
9. 3 Tbsp cooking oil
10. Salt to taste

Method

1. In a small bowl, add water to the corn or tapioca starch and mix until you get a slurry.
2. Mix the soy sauce, fish sauce and sugar into the slurry. Set aside.
3. In a frying pan or wok, add the oil and heat over medium-low heat.
4. Add the ginger and fry until fragrant but not brown, about 30 seconds.
5. Increase the heat to medium.
6. Add the water chestnuts or Daylily tubers and stir fry for about 5 minutes.
7. Add the Daylily buds.

8. Stir your starch-slurry to a consistent mixture before pouring it over the ingredients in the pan.
9. Stir fry until the ingredients are coated in the sauce.
10. Add salt to taste (optional).
11. Serve immediately with rice.

Daylily Root Bundt Cake

Ingredients

1. 2 c Daylily tubers, washed and shredded
2. 2 c all-purpose flour
3. 2 eggs
4. 1/4 c lemon juice
5. 1/2 c maple syrup
6. 1/4 c honey
7. 1/2 tsp salt
8. 1/2 tsp baking powder
9. 1 tsp baking soda
10. 1 tsp ground cinnamon
11. 1/2 c + 2 Tbsp oil

For the icing:
1. 1 c powdered sugar
2. 1 Tbsp milk or water
3. 1/2 tsp vanilla extract

Method

1. Preheat the oven to 350°F.
2. Grease and lightly flour a bundt pan.
3. In a bowl, toss the tubers in the lemon juice.
4. In a mixer bowl, sift flour, salt, baking powder, baking soda and cinnamon.
5. In another bowl, whisk the eggs, oil, maple syrup and honey together
6. Start the mixer on low speed with the dry ingredients in the mixer.

7. With the mixer running on low, add the wet ingredients to the dry ingredients.
8. Stop the mixer, scrape the sides down, then resume mixing at medium speed for 30 seconds.
9. Stop the mixer and fold the shredded tubers into the batter.
10. Pour the batter into a greased Bundt pan and bake for 30-40 minutes, or until the cake is firm and golden.
11. Remove from the oven and allow it to cool for about 10 minutes before inverting the pan onto a serving plate.
12. Allow the cake to cool completely.
13. Make the icing by whisking the powdered sugar into milk or water and vanilla extract.
14. Drizzle over the cake before serving.

- *Recipe by the3foragers.blogspot.com*

Other Uses

According to Plants for a Future (http://pfaf.org), the tough, dried foliage can be woven into cords and used to make footwear.

Medicinally, Daylily tubers have shown to have anti-microbial activity. In China, the flowers are used as a painkiller for women during childbirth. In Korea, it is used to treat various medical conditions, including jaundice, constipation and pneumonia. The roots, when boiled to make a tea, is used as a diuretic.

7 HOSTA

Hosta Montana

Native to Northeast Asia, Hosta is now a widely cultivated, shade-tolerant herbaceous perennial. From the Asparagaceae family, Hostas are also known as plantain lilies and as *giboshi* in Japan.

I chose to include Hostas to the list because this attractive plant is one of the few plants that will generally grow in shade. It is also not generally recognized in North America as edible. In Japan however, Hostas have long been used as a food source. According to the Montreal Botanical Garden, all species are edible but I cannot definitively verify this assertion.

According to ethno-botanist and BBC presenter James Wong, *H. montana* and *H. sieboldii* are the preferred varieties for consumption because known for their tender and less bitter leaves vegetables. *H. plantaginea* is sometimes planted for flower consumption as well as honey production. *H. fortunei* is said to be the tastiest species but more importantly, it is fast-growing and more sun-tolerant than most other varieties.

Cultivation

Hostas need a period of cold weather but are otherwise fairly adaptable perennials. They will grow in Zones 3-9 but tend not to thrive in arid climates. They grow well in moist soils in partial shade. Some varieties may also be able to adapt to direct sun if grown in cooler, north-facing areas where there is good soil moisture.

Hostas prefer slightly acidic to neutral (pH 5.5 to 6.5) well-draining soils with high organic matter. While Hostas grow in shady spots, full shade will stunt their growth. Choose a planting location that has morning sun exposure. Gold, yellow and white leaf varieties are more tolerant of sun exposure while blue varieties are more shade tolerant.

Hostas are usually planted using potted starter plants. Before planting, prepare the Hosta planting bed by working in as much as 6 inches of organic matter, which can consist of composted manure, compost or leaf mold.

Prepare a hole wide enough to account for horizontal root expansion to a foot deep. Carefully remove the Hosta from its pot, shaking off any loose soil before planting. Position the Hosta at a height similar to the one it was growing at in its container. This should be where the bottom leaves appear just above the ground level. If you plant the crown a little above the ground level, it will be a little easier to harvest the unfurled leaves or "hostons".

Water well immediately after planting. To maintain, water at least 1 inch of water per week, more in hot weather or if you are planting in sandy soil. It's best to water on a regular schedule early in the day to reduce moisture loss through evaporation. Signs of the lack of watering include the leaves drooping, changing color or showing sign of "burn".

Add a 2-4 inch layer of organic mulch when the soil warms up in late spring to early summer to help to maintain soil moisture and temperature. The mulch will also help to keep weeds down. Be sure to keep the plant's central crown clear.

If you like the shoots, you can use the trick that some Japanese growers use -- cover Hotsa crowns with several inches of straw mulch in early spring to encourage new shoots to produce extra growth.

Potential Problems

Unfortunately, Hostas can suffer from a host of pests and diseases namely, slugs, snails, deer, voles and a foliar disease, Anthracnose. Smooth but irregular holes along the leaf veins or edges and shiny slime trails on and around the plants indicate slug or snail attacks. Setting out dishes of beer around the plants will help to trap and drown slugs. Otherwise, ducks are a good, natural way to get rid of them.

Rabbits will clean cut leaves and leave distinctive droppings while deer will usually consume the leaves but leave the stalks intact. Voles will usually attack from below, consuming the roots which will cause the plants to wilt or collapse from the lack of support. Fencing will help to keep these pests out.

Hostas' most common foliar disease is Anthracnose, which is characterized by irregularly shaped white or tan spots with a brown border. The leaves usually become torn or tattered and the spots may lose their centers. Having good plant spacing with good air circulation will help to prevent this problem because the disease thrives in warm, wet conditions.

Harvesting

The shoots, leaf stems, leaves and flowers of Hostas are edible but the hoston is considered the best part of the Hosta and emerges in spring. The older stems, leaves and short leaves that grow around the base are also edible but tend to be bitter. The young shoots are therefore preferred for their mild taste and soft texture.

It's best to harvest the leaves in the morning, when their moisture content is highest. The best way to harvest hostons is by holding them firmly near the base and snapping off the ones on the clump edges at the base. Snapping them off at the base will help to keep the leaves together instead of the individual leaves falling apart.

If the plant is established, you can harvest the entire first flush of leaves without killing the plant. This process will produce a second flush of fresh leaves. If in doubt, harvest no more than half the amount of leaves. But, if you want to err on the side of caution, leave two-thirds of the leaves in place.

All's not lost if you are too late to harvest the hostons -- the open leaves can be cooked as a spinach or green vegetable substitute. Later in the season, the flower buds and flowers can be consumed. The flowers are usually used as decorative garnishes. Consume as soon as possible after harvesting. Once harvested, Hostas dry out quickly. Wrap the stems in moistened paper towels and place it in a plastic bag, standing upright in the fridge to prolong the harvest.

While edible Hostas are safe for human consumption, note that they are toxic to cats and dogs.

Propagation

Hotas can be divided in spring or fall. However, lifting and dividing Hostas will slow their maturity by as much as several years. Therefore, unless you have a reason for doing so, it is generally not a good idea to divide your Hosta patch until it reaches a space limit and growth starts to slow down.

There is about a four-week window in spring and in fall to divide your Hostas. In spring, the time when the Hosta eyes are appearing but before the leaves start to unfurl is the period when you can divide them. In fall, the time to divide

Hostas is when the weather turns cool and moist, which is usually around September in colder climates and in late October in warmer areas.

The soil should be moist when you lift and divide your Hostas. If it is dry, water the area well the day before you plan to divide the plant. Depending on how large your clump is, you can cut the outermost eyes without touching the main clump and propagate it that way.

If you have a large clump that you want to divide, sink a clean, straight spade deeply (8-18" depending on the cultivar) into the ground around the clump such that it is far enough away from the clump that you do not sever too many roots.

Use the spade to cut the clump from underneath. To make cleanup easier, place your divided clumps on a tarp close by. If you have a large Hosta patch of 30 or so eyes, you can divide by cutting out a clumps, half, a third or a quarter in size. In any method, avoid slicing into the eyes. Some cultivars can be pulled apart but most will need to be cut apart.

Food Uses

Hostas can be eaten raw or cooked and has its own flavor, which I liken to pea-asparagus-lettucey. The best hostons are ones with plump white stems and young leaves that are still fresh but yellowish-green. Small hostons are good fried or stir-fried while the larger ones are better as a blanched vegetable. Note though, that Hostas will produce a sliminess when cooked.

The flowers that have not quite opened will be the most tender. Their smell is fruity and can be paired with melons or a fruit salad.

Recipes

Creamy Potato and Hosta Soup

Ingredients

1. 4 c milk (using whole milk will result in a creamier soup)
2. 1 c or more chicken or vegetable stock or water
3. 1/2 c white onion, peeled and chopped
4. 1/2 c carrots, thinly sliced
5. 3/4 c celery, thinly sliced
6. 1/2 c Hosta stems, thinly sliced
7. 5 potatoes, peeled and cubed
8. 1 Tbsp butter
9. 1-2 Tbsp flour
10. 1 1/2 tsp salt or to taste
11. 1 tsp ground black pepper or to taste

Method

1. In a stockpot, melt the butter over medium-low heat.
2. Sprinkle and whisk in the flour until you achieve a smooth paste.
3. Keep stirring until the flour stops smelling raw, about 5 minutes.
4. Slowly stir in the stock or water,
5. Keep stirring until you achieve an even consistency.
6. Add the onions, carrots, potatoes, celery and seasonings.
7. Cover and lower the heat to a simmer until the vegetables become soft, about 1-2 hours. You may

need to add more water or stock if the liquid reduces too much.

8. Stir in the milk and the Hostas.
9. Cover and simmer for about ten more minutes.
10. Serve hot.

Crispy Hosta Shoots

Ingredients

1. 2 c all-purpose flour
2. 4 eggs
3. 10 stalks Hosta shoots, cleaned and cut into 2-inch pieces
4. 2 Tbsp seasoned salt or your favorite seasoning to taste
5. Oil for frying

Method

1. In a mixing bowl, combine the flour and seasonings. Mix well.
2. In another bowl, beat the eggs and add the Hosta shoot segments.
3. Stir to completely cover the shoots in egg.
4. Remove the Hostas from the eggs and allow the excess egg to drip off.
5. Toss the Hosta shoots in the flour until completely coated.
6. Remove from the flour and allow the excess flour to fall off.
7. In a large heavy skillet, heat the oil over medium heat.
8. Test the oil temperature by adding a bit of egg into the oil. If it bubbles immediately, the oil is hot enough. If it bubbles vigorously and starts to burn, the oil is too hot.

9. Gently add the breaded Hosta shoots into the hot oil, making sure not to crowd the skillet.
10. Stir and fry until golden-brown.
11. Remove from the oil and drain the shoots on a paper towel-lined plate.
12. Repeat the process until all the Hosta shoots are fried.
13. Serve hot.

Crustless Hosta Quiche

Ingredients

1. 1 lb fresh Hosta shoots, cleaned and cut into 1/2-inch segments
2. 4 eggs
3. 1 1/2 c milk
4. 3 Tbsp butter
5. 3 Tbsp all-purpose flour
6. 1/2 c mild Cheddar cheese or cheese of your choice, shredded
7. 1/4 c dry bread crumbs
8. 1/2 tsp salt or to taste + 1 Tbsp salt

Method

1. In a stock pot, bring water to a boil. Add about 1 Tbsp of salt to the boiling water.
2. Gently drop the Hostas pieces into the boiling water and blanch for about 3 minutes before removing from the water and running them under cold water.
3. Preheat the oven to 400°F.
4. In a saucepan, melt the butter over medium heat.
5. Mix in the flour and salt.
6. Add the milk and lower the heat.
7. Stir and cook until thickened.
8. In a mixing bowl, beat the eggs and slowly mix a small amount of the milk-mixture into the eggs to temper the eggs.
9. Once tempered, add the egg-mixture to the milk, stirring the whole time.

10. Stir in the cheese and Hosta pieces.
11. Pour the mixture into a baking pan lined with aluminum foil.
12. Sprinkle the breadcrumbs evenly on top.
13. Bake for about 30 minutes or until a knife or skewer inserted in the center comes out clean.
14. Serve hot.

Other Uses

Hostas can also be used as a slow-growing groundcover.

8 LOVAGE

Lovage Plant

While the origins of Lovage (*Levisticum officinale*) is disputed, it is believed to have originated somewhere in or between southeastern Europe and southwestern Asia. Belonging to the Apiaceae family, records of its cultivation for its culinary and medicinal properties dates as far back as 14th century Europe.

Sometimes also known as Love Persley, Sea Parsley or "Maggi Plant" for its flavor that is reminiscent of Maggi soup seasoning, this perennial grows between 3-6 feet tall. The entire plant, from its roots to its seeds are edible.

The round, ribbed, hollow stem branches near the top and grows from a short, thick rootstock. Compound, opposite leaves are dark green and glossy, decreasing in size as it grows towards the top. The ovate, tooth leaflets have a fragrance similar to that of celery and the plant is often used as a celery-substitute. The flowers are small and pale yellow. They are arranged in compound umbels which are normally 1.5-4 inches across. It produces a seed 1/2 -inch long.

While not an uncommon food-plant in parts of Europe, this fairly attractive plant is not generally recognized as an edible plant in North America.

Cultivation

Lovage grows best as a perennial in Zones 3-8. While Lovage will tolerate most soils except heavy clay, it grows best in a sunny location with slightly alkaline to slightly acidic (pH of 5.0-7.6) well-draining or sandy, loamy soil.

Note that Lovage will grow big and tall over time so in the Northern Hemisphere, it is a good idea to plant it in the Northern part of the garden, where it will not eventually shade surrounding shorter plants.

Plant Lovage seeds in late summer or fall. Before planting, prepare the soil by spreading an inch of compost and an inch of peat moss on the soil surface. Double the amounts if you have heavy clay soil. Use a broad fork or spade to loosen the soil and to incorporate the compost and peat moss. Rake the bed smooth.

Direct sow the seeds about 1/4-1/2 inch deep and 6 inches apart. Using your hands, gently press on the surface of the soil to firm it up, but do not water or apply winter mulch. Allow the seeds to overwinter and germinate in spring.

In spring, when the seedlings are about 4 inches tall, transplant or thin them until they are about 2-3 feet apart. Water until the soil is evenly moist but not wet. Apply a 2-inch layer of organic mulch like shredded leaves or pine needles to help to keep the weeds down and the soil temperature and moisture more consistent. Water regularly, especially in hot or arid conditions.

In late fall, cut the plant down to about 1-foot high and cover it with protective mulch. The mulch should be deep enough such that it covers the plant by another foot for winter protection. Lovage needs top growth to help to ensure that it survives the winter so do not cut the plant down to the ground to overwinter.

In spring, remove the winter mulch and side dress with an organic fertilizer like fully decomposed manure. Add fresh mulch and water regularly. Lovage should be fertilized at least once a year.

Potential Problems

Lovage plants are prone to aphid, leaf miner and fungi attacks. Leaf miner attacks can be distinguished by white-colored burrowing spots on certain leaves. Remove and destroy any leaves that exhibit signs of attack.

Aphids are usually most apparent on the underside of the leaves or on the stem. However, they may appear on any part of the plant. You can get rid of them by hosing them off with a strong spray of water, or by applying insecticidal soap.

Improving air-circulation by giving the plants adequate space will help to reduce the incidence of fungal attacks. I have not tried this myself but according to howstuffworks.com, you can also make a baking soda preventative spray by shaking a mix of 2 teaspoons baking soda in 2 quarts water with 1/2 teaspoon corn oil and spraying the mix on susceptible plants after a rain.

Harvesting

You can harvest the Lovage leaves in the first year, once the plants have become established. Avoid washing the leaves, which will cause the plant to lose its aromatic oils. In the second year, you can harvest entire branches.

To harvest, choose a cool, dry morning, after the dew has dried but before the hot afternoon sun starts to scorch the plant. The leaves can be harvested any time of the year while stems are best consumed young.

Lovage produces large seed heads in late summer, which can be collected by allowing the heads to dry on the plant before collection. You can also bag the ripening seed to capture them that way. The seeds are sweeter in flavor than the leaves and can be used as a celery seed substitute (which in turn, is often used as a salt-substitute).

The roots should be harvested only in fall. Wash and cut it into small pieces before using it, or dry the pieces on a screen to preserve it. Store the dried roots in a cool, dry place away from light.

Lovage is best used fresh but can be dried for storage. For drying purposes, it's best to collect the stems with leaves before the plants start flowering. Dry by tying cuttings in small bunches and hanging them upside down in a dark, undisturbed area with good air circulation.

Once dried, strip the leaves off the stems and store them in an air-tight container in a cool, dry place. Lovage can also be stored by blanching it very quickly in boiling water then immediately immersing it in ice water. Dry and freeze in freezer bags.

Propagation

Lovage propagates on its own easily from seed through its ripened fruit seeds. If you want to prevent the plant from overrunning the garden, sever the fruit-bearing branches before the seeds ripen and fall to the ground.

It is a fairly long-lived perennial, usually surviving for around eight years. However, like most other things, they tend to lose vigor as they age. It is therefore a good idea to divide your plants every 3-4 years. The best time to divide is in early spring or in late fall when the plant is dormant. To divide, separate an outer section that includes an eye or bud, as well as roots, of a mature plant. Plant the divisions in a new location at least 2 feet apart.

Food Uses

Lovage is similar to celery in flavor but more complex, with hints of parsley and earthiness. The young leaves are mild enough to be used whole in salads but will also withstand being slow-cooked in stews and soups.

If sectioned off, the hollow stem can be used like a straw for drinks like Bloody Mary, which call for a celery flavor. The stems can also be candied for a treat. The seeds can be used ground or whole, added to candies, meats, stews, breads, crackers, cheese or sauces. Like capers, Lovage seeds can be used for flavoring pickles.

Dried roots can be used as a condiment. Once the outer skin is peeled off, the fresh roots can be grated and used in salads, to make teas and can be preserved in honey. To make a stimulating tea or tisane, steep one teaspoon of fresh or finely shredded dried Lovage roots in a cup of boiling water.

Recipes

Cole Slaw with Lovage Seeds

Ingredients

1. 2 lbs cabbage, coarsely chopped
2. 1 c carrot, peeled and shredded
3. 3/4 c sugar or to taste
4. 3/4 c cider vinegar
5. 1 tsp Lovage seeds
6. 1 tsp garlic powder
7. Salt to taste

Method

1. In a mixing bowl, mix the cabbage and carrot.
2. In a separate bowl, mix all the other ingredients.
3. Pour the seasoning mixture over the cabbage-mix.
4. Mix well.
5. Chill and allow the cole slaw to marinate for a few hours before serving.
6. Serve cold.

Egg Salad with Lovage

Ingredients

1. 6 large eggs, hard-boiled and peeled
2. 1/4 c Lovage leaves, finely chopped
3. 2 sprigs of chives or green onions, finely chopped (optional)
4. 4-6 Tbsp mayonnaise
5. 1/8 tsp ground mustard or to taste (optional)
6. 1/4 tsp Lovage seeds (optional)
7. Salt and pepper to taste (optional)

Method

1. In a mixing bowl, mash the hard-boiled eggs.
2. Add all the other ingredients to the mashed eggs.
3. Mix well.
4. Serve between bread slices as a sandwich or on a bed of lettuce.

Potato and Lovage Soup

Ingredients

1. 2 medium potatoes, peeled and diced
2. 4 six-inch stalks of Lovage, chopped
3. 1 small onion, peeled and chopped
4. 4 garlic cloves, peeled and minced
5. 1 Tbsp butter
6. 2 bay leaf and sprigs of thyme and parsley
7. 7 cups Water (or chicken broth)
8. Salt and pepper to taste

Method

1. In a stock pot, heat the butter over medium heat.
2. Add the onions and Lovage.
3. Reduce the heat to medium-low, stirring until the onions and Lovage become tender, around 10 minutes.
4. Add the potatoes, garlic, seasonings and water.
5. Bring to a boil then cover and simmer until the vegetables become very tender.
6. Remove from the heat and puree the soup with a food processor or blender.
7. Serve hot.

Lemon Lovage Baked Chicken

Ingredients

1. 1 whole chicken, quartered or 4 whole chicken legs
2. 1 lemon, sliced
3. 1 onion, peeled and chopped
4. 2-3 carrots, peeled and diced
5. 2 medium potatoes, peeled and diced (optional)
6. 1 c Lovage leaves and stems, chopped
7. Lovage seeds, salt and pepper to taste
8. 1 Tbsp butter

Method

1. Preheat oven to 350°F..
2. Lay some of the Lovage on the bottom of baking pan lined with foil.
3. Tuck the lemon slices and Lovage leaves under the skin of the chicken.
4. Arrange the chicken in a single layer in the pan.
5. Add the carrots and potatoes around the chicken pieces.
6. Add dabs of butter on your ingredients.
7. Sprinkle the seasonings evenly on the chicken and vegetables.
8. Cover with aluminum foil and bake for 30 minutes.
9. Using oven mitts, remove the foil and bake uncovered for an additional 30 minutes or until the chicken is done (usually when the juices run clear).
10. (Optional) Broil for 3-5 minutes until the skin turns golden-brown.
11. Serve hot with your choice of sides.

Lovage Ice-Cream

Ingredients

1. About 2 c of Lovage leaves and stems, roughly chopped
2. 2 2/3 c whole milk
3. 1 1/2 c heavy cream
4. 3/4 c sugar
5. 1/4 c corn syrup
6. 1 1/2 Tbsp cornstarch
7. 4 Tbsp cream cheese, softened
8. 3 wide strips of lime zest
9. 1/4 tsp kosher salt

Method

1. In a large mixing bowl, whisk the cream cheese until smooth.
2. In a separate small bowl, make a slurry by mixing a few tablespoons of the milk to the cornstarch.
3. In a large saucepan, heat the remaining milk, cream, sugar, corn syrup and salt on medium-high.
4. Bring the milk mixture to a boil then lower the heat to a simmer for about 5 minutes.
5. Remove from heat and whisk in the cornstarch slurry.
6. Add the Lovage and lime zest.
7. Return to saucepan to the stove and bring it to a boil over medium heat, stirring constantly.
8. Keep stirring until the mixture is slightly thickened, about 1 minute.

9. Remove from heat and pour the mixture over the cream cheese, whisking until thoroughly combined.
10. Cover and allow it to cool before refrigerating overnight.
11. Pass the mixture through a fine mesh strainer and process in an ice cream maker.

- *Recipe by blossomtostem.net*

Other Uses

Historically, Lovage has been used medicinally for the digestive and respiratory systems. It has been used to cure poor appetite, indigestion, bronchitis, gas and colic as well as urinary tract problems. Lovage is also said to stimulate menstruation and alleviate menstrual pain.

A historical recipe for coughs and lung and chest complaints calls for 0.2 oz Lovage, 0.2 oz sage, 0.7 oz fennel steeped in 2 cups of wine for 1-2 days. Strained, a small glass of this infusion was heated and drunk after meals. Heating the wine was not necessary if the cough is mild. **Consult your medical professional before using any herbal remedies.**

As a companion plant, Lovage planted in small patches is said to help to promote vigorous growth in potatoes or other root vegetables.

9 LUPINE

Lupinus angustifolius

WARNING: There are two kinds of Lupines. All parts of certain kinds of wild Lupines are 100% *poisonous* to both humans and livestock. Make sure that the variety you are planting is specifically labelled as one of the edible varieties.

Lupines are believed to have originated in Egypt before it was spread around the world by cultivators for their many uses including its food-use. There are hundreds of species of Lupines, also known as Lupins, all of which fall under the legume family, Fabaceae. Lupines are also sometimes known as "Wolf Beans", probably because of Lupine's tendency to grow and thrive in remote areas where wolves roam.

Like Amaranth, Lupine can range from wild to cultivated, annual or perennial (although most are perennial), bushy or tall, ranging in heights of between 1 to 20 feet. Unlike

Amaranth however, not all Lupines are safe to eat. Wild varieties (which usually have blue or purple flowers) are toxic to both humans and livestock so be sure to remove and wild varieties from your pasture.

There are also bitter and sweet Lupines, depending on the amount of alkaloids they contain. Bitter Lupines have a higher alkaloid content and are more common in the Mediterranean areas while sweet Lupines are more commonly found in North America.

Edible Lupines are attractive plants and in North America, they are not readily recognizable as edible. Lupine seeds can not only be be used as a high fiber, high protein, low-fat food crop but as a fodder crop as well. As an additional advantage, they can also be used a green manure and as a nitrogen fixer. Its long tap root lends itself to being a soil aerator as well.

Cultivation

Lupines need a period of cold to thrive and therefore grow in the cooler climates of Zones 4-9. They will grow in sandy to loamy soils but prefer moist though well-drained, average to poor soil. They do best in partial shade or in a sunny location, in neutral to slightly acidic soil and will not tolerate shady locations.

For an earlier start, you can start indoors 6-8 weeks before the last frost date. To plant from seed, pre-soak the seeds in warm water for 24 hours. Stratify the seeds by sandwiching them between moist paper towels and putting them in a ziplock bag in the fridge for 7 days. Germination will usually occur in about two weeks. Move the seedlings outdoors when they are large enough to handle.

You can also sow the Lupine seeds directly into your bed after all danger of frost has passed. Remove all weeds and vegetation from the garden bed and add some bonemeal to the soil before planting. The seeds should be planted 1-2" deep and covered lightly with soil. Space the seeds 12-14" apart.

Evenly water daily to keep the soil moist but not wet. Mulch around the plants to help maintain soil moisture and temperature consistency. When the plants have matured, fertilize with a high phosphorus but low nitrogen fertilizer like bat guano or worm castings.

Potential Problems

Lupines generally do not suffer from many pests other than aphid infestation, which you can remove by spraying off or by applying insecticidal soap.

Some garden Lupines are also susceptible to Lupine Anthracnose, which is a serious disease caused by a type of fungus. In the initial stages, you'll see young shoots gradually dying. The fungus later attacks the larger branches, causing the leaves to brown and fall off. If not controlled, it will kill the plant.

Prevent the spread by not watering Lupines overhead. In the initial stages, you might be able to spray a fungicide to kill the fungus. Once severely infected, you'll need to completely remove and destroy the plant to prevent the disease from spreading.

Harvesting

To harvest the seeds, allow the Lupines to bloom and set seed in late summer. Do not deadhead the faded blooms because this will stop the plant from forming seeds. Start checking the seeds when the pods, which look like pea pods, start to yellow and turn brown. The seeds should be hard and may sometimes rattle in the pod when you harvest.

Choose a cool, dry day, after the morning dew has dried, to harvest the seeds by picking the pods. Place paper towels or newspapers on your work area and open your pods over them. Remove the seeds and spread them on the newspapers or paper towels to allow them to dry completely over two or three days. Store in an airtight container in a cool, dark, dry place.

Propagation

Perennial Lupines can also be propagated by cuttings or divisions although because of its long taproot, propagating by division is seldom done. Basal cuttings are best done in mid-spring. Prepare your planting medium by filling a container with moistened coarse building or masonry sand (but not fine play sand). Insert 3-4 wooden or bamboo skewers at regular intervals along the edge of the growing container. The ends of skewers should reach 2-3 inches above the planted Lupine cutting.

Using a clean, sharp knife or blade, cut a stem, including its heel (the small part of the original stem that is attached to the basal end) off a mature Lupine. In one hand, grip the top of the stem and use the index finger and thumb of your other hand to strip all but the uppermost leaves off the Lupine stem. Cut the remaining leaves horizontally in half and stick the cutting in the sand such that the sand is firmly around the stem.

Make a makeshift miniature greenhouse by covering the planting container with a plastic bag or film with the wooden stakes propping the plastic above the cutting. You might need to use a rubber band to keep the plastic in place and to seal the cuttings in the mini greenhouse. Place the cutting in a warm, bright location but away from direct sunlight.

Allow the cutting to breathe by removing the plastic for about 30 minutes every day to help to ventilate the mini greenhouse. This is also a good time to moisten the sand if it feels dry. Replace the plastic and repeat the process every day for about 3-4 weeks. After this time, very gently tug on the cutting to see if it has rooted.

Once rooted, you can transplant the cutting into a biodegradable pot filled with good potting soil. The Lupine is ready to be planted outside when it is big enough to not be lost in the garden. Lupines do not like to be transplanted so plant the entire biodegradable pot in its final location outside.

Propagation by dividing should be carried out in spring, never in fall, which will kill the plant. Dividing Lupine is a little different. Instead of cutting into the crown, carefully lift the plant with the top foliage intact and divide the roots into sections.

The number of sections the plant yields will depend on the root size but you should generally get 4 sections. Replant each section with as much roots as possible in your chosen location. Once planted, water them well and immediately. Keep the new plant well-watered to make sure that they don't dry out in this critical stage.

Food Uses

Again, do NOT consume random Lupines. Wild varieties are toxic. Purchase only edible varieties from reliable sources.

The main edible species of Lupines are *Lupinus albus* (Mediterranean region) and *Lupinus mutabilis* in Latin America. Sometimes known as "Lupini beans" in Italy or "Zbib" in Lebanon, they may also be known as Ludmilla, Tarwi and Nabah Cairo.

Lupin beans are most commonly consumed in Mediterranean countries as well as in parts of the Middle East and South America. They can be eaten with or without the tough skin/shell. The beans are often kept in brine and consumed as an appetizer.

According to the "Molecular Nutrition & Food Research" journal published by the University of Milan, neither cooking nor soaking is required for sweet Lupine beans. However, a study by the same university recommended in the "Journal of Agricultural and Food Chemistry", that both sweet and bitter Lupini beans should undergo the debittering process before consumption to reduce any possible toxicity. Bitter Lupine beans may also be consumed raw or cooked as long as the toxic bitter alkaloids are removed first.

Processing Bitter Lupines

Bitter Lupines contain high levels of alkaloids that can be poisonous. There are a few methods of removing the alkaloids. Some soak the beans until the toxins are removed, before adding salt and boiling them; while others soak the beans overnight before pre-boiling.

Avoid using table salt for the brine because it tends to leave a milky white sediment in the jars. Use canning salt instead. You can soak the beans in non-porous containers like glass or metal but avoid soaking them in plastic containers, which may absorb the toxins before leaching them out at a later point.

Method 1

This method produces a firmer final product.

1. In a large metal colander, pick and remove any discolored, partly shelled or shriveled beans.
2. Rinse the beans under cool, clean water thoroughly.
3. In a large enough stock pot, cover the beans with enough cool, clean water (use about 1 gallon per 2 lbs of beans).
4. Soak for 24 hours.
5. You may notice an odor being emitted from the beans. This odor is caused by the beans' toxins, which will eventually dissipate.
6. Drain and rinse the beans well with cool, clean water.

7. Wash the pot and lid with warm soapy water to remove any residual toxins that might have adhered to the pot's surface.

8. Add the beans back to the cleaned pot and fill it with the same amount of cool, clean water.

9. To make a brine soak, add 1 tablespoon of canning salt per quart of water used.

10. Cover the pot and refrigerate the soaking beans overnight.

11. Drain and rinse the beans twice a day, washing the pot with warm soapy water during each draining.

12. Return the beans to a fresh brine solution and refrigerate after each rinse.

13. Repeat the draining, rinsing and washing regiment until the bitterness is gone. This usually takes 9-14 days. After the fifth day, you can start testing the beans by nibbling on them but not swallowing.

14. When the beans stop being bitter, they can be added to recipes or consumed immediately.

15. The beans will last several weeks in the fridge.

Method 2

1. In a non-porous pot, soak the beans in cool, clean water for 24 hours.
2. Drain and rinse the beans in clean, fresh water and return the beans to a fresh pot of water.
3. Bring the beans and water to a boil.
4. Skim off any dark foam that forms on the surface.
5. Allow the beans to continue simmering for 40 minutes and continue skimming off any dark foam from the surface.
6. Remove the beans from the heat.
7. Drain and rinse the beans with clean, fresh water.
8. Transfer the beans to a clean non-porous bowl and cover them with fresh water.
9. Cover and allow the beans to soak overnight in the fridge.
10. Repeat the draining, rinsing and soaking process every day for at least 7 days or until the bitterness is gone.
11. Once the bitterness is removed, drain and rinse the beans before storing them in clean containers covered in fresh water.
12. Add plenty of salt (at least 1/4 cup per quart of water) before storing covered in the fridge.
13. Note that the longer the beans soak in the brine, the softer they will become.
14. If it is too salty, rinse the excess salt off before use.

Prepared Lupini beans are good drizzled with olive oil, fresh crushed garlic, parsley, pepper or even with Japanese soba sauce or tamari. Middle Eastern recipes call for the addition of lime juice and cumin.

You can eat the beans with the chewy skins or bite into the skin with your front teeth to pop the bean into your mouth. Try not to turn the bean into a little projectile!

Recipes

Lupini Ceviche

Ingredients

1. 1 c Cherry tomatoes, halved
2. 2 c prepared Lupini beans, cooked
3. 1 Tbsp Parsley
4. 2 Tbsp Red onion, diced finely
5. 1/2 Sweet potato, cooked, peeled and cubed
6. 1 tsp Aji amarillo paste
7. 1/2 c Lime juice
8. 1 Tbsp olive oil
9. 1 salt to taste

Method

1. In a bowl, combine all the ingredients except the tomatoes and sweet potatoes.
2. Mix the tomatoes in just before serving.
3. Serve with the sweet potatoes on the side.

- *Recipe by Que Rica Vida*

Lupini Hummus

Ingredients

1. 3 c prepared Lupini beans, rinsed and drained
2. 4 cloves of garlic, peeled and minced
3. 3 Tbsp lemon juice or to taste
4. 1/2 cup olive oil
5. Salt and black pepper to taste

Method

1. In a food processor, add all the ingredients except the olive oil.
2. Pulse until mixed. Stop the food processor and scrape the sides down frequently.
3. While pulsing, slowly add the olive oil.
4. Grind until smooth.
5. Serve with pita bread or as a dip.

Other Uses

Besides being used for food, Lupine species like *Lupinus angustifolius* can also be used as fodder and as green manure. In less developed areas, it may be used to attract wildlife like deer, turkeys, quail and other game which, in an emergency, can be hunted for their meat.

If you have livestock or poultry, it may also be used as fodder. Consult your veterinarian if you intend to add cultivated Lupine (not the toxic wild varieties) to your livestock's forage. According to "The Great Soviet Encyclopedia" (1979), the best time for harvesting Lupine for fodder is when the pods become shiny.

Lupines can also be used as a green manure to help to boost your prepper garden. "The Great Soviet Encyclopedia" (1979) describes how Lupine can be planted as a green manure crop: "Washington lupine is cultivated in fallow fields (for green manure) and undersown in spring fields. This process is followed by crop rotation. Additional plantings are useful as intermediary green manure crops among winter rye; sowing is done in the autumn before snowfall, in the winter while the snow is on the ground, or in early spring. The green mass is most often plowed under for potatoes (in the spring of the second year). To obtain seeds and green manure, non-rotated sections are also planted, and the crop is mown annually and taken away to fertilize other fields."

10 Nasturtium

Nasturtiums

Tropaeolum is more commonly known as Nasturtium and is native to South and Central America. Although they are normally grown as decorative annual garden plants, they are technically herbaceous perennials in warmer climates. These fast-growing plants are easy to grow and the entire *Tropaeolum majus* plant, from the stems to the flowers to the seeds, is edible.

Literally meaning "nose twist" in Latin, Nasturtium belongs to the Tropaeolaceae family and does *not* belong to the genus *Nasturtium,* which includes water cress. Nasturtium is also sometimes known as Indian Cress, Monk Cress or Garden Nasturtium.

Nasturtium's green, peltate leaves are large and nearly circular, with a slightly lobed margin. They range between 1.2-5.9 inches in diameter, and have several veins that radiate from each leaf. The leaves grow from trailing stems that are 3 or more feet long. The five-petaled flowers are 1-3 inches in diameter, with eight stamens, and have long nectar spur at the the back, about 1 inch long. The most common colors are orange, yellow, cream and red as well as shades in between. The three-segmented fruit that the flower produces is about an inch wide. Each segment produces a single large seed about an inch long.

Nasturtium is not commonly viewed as an edible plant but makes the list for its versatility, deliciousness, attractiveness and ease of cultivation.

Cultivation

Nasturtium is a perennial in Zones 9-10 but can be grown easily with little care as an annual in cooler climates. They grow best in full sun but in areas where summers are hot, it is best to grow them in part-shade.

They like cool, damp well-draining soil that is not too rich. If you have very sandy soil, add about an inch of compost to help to hold in some moisture. There is no need to fertilize the plant further. If grown in nitrogen-rich soil, Nasturtiums will produce a lot green foliage and few flowers. Avoid this situation if you're growing Nasturtiums as annuals and need to save seeds.

Nasturtiums are easily started from seed. To sow directly, press the seeds into a planting bed free of weeds and other plants. When all danger of frost has passed, plant the seeds about 1/2-inch deep, 10-12 inches apart in the ground. In short-season areas, you can start the seeds indoors.

Nasturtiums do not like being transplanted and should be started in peat pots which can be planted directly into the garden when the roots start showing through the pot's drainage hole. However, I do not think it is worth the hassle, since Nasturtiums germinate and mature so quickly. When I planted them in Zone 4, they could be direct-sown and still complete the entire life-cycle before first frost.

Keep the bed well-watered after sowing. The seeds will normally germinate in about 2 weeks. If you are growing trailing varieties on a trellis, you will need to tie them up because they do not produce tendrils. Cut the plants back if they suffer in the summer heat. They'll regrow and flower again when the weather cools.

Problems

Nasturtiums are fairly trouble-free but the new leaves and flowers may be attacked by aphids. Remove the aphids by spraying them off with water, or by applying insecticidal soap.

Harvesting

Nasturtium can be harvested for their flowers, flower buds and leaves. Both young and old leaves are edible but the young ones taste better. Choose a cool, dry morning to harvest, after the morning dew has dried and when the flowers have just opened.

The leaves and flowers will be more pungent in taste if they have been heat-stressed. If the whole flower is too strong for your taste, you can eat just the petals. Wash and dry the leaves and flowers gently for immediate use. They can also be stored in a plastic bag in the fridge.

Nasturtium seeds are usually harvested and consumed while still green to be used as a seasoning. Prune the green seed pods from the plant when they are round and plump. While the seeds can be eaten raw, they tend to be very strong when consumed this way. Pickling in brine helps to mellow the flavor.

Propagation

Nasturtiums can be started from basal cuttings but is best and most easily and quickly started from seed. It is hard to harvest seeds that have perfectly ripened on the plant.

Instead, you can harvest, brush clean and save dried, mature seed pods that have fallen to the ground or, you can collect the green seeds from the plant. The color of the seeds does not seem to matter as much as the seed-size when it comes to germination. Save the larger seeds for replanting, which seem to yield better germination results.

Spread the mature seed pods on a paper towel and allow them to dry out completely in a sunny, undisturbed location.

Shake the seeds a little everyday to ensure even drying. Once dry, you can crack the seed pods open. Remove the seeds and store them in an air-tight container in a cool, dry place until you are ready to plant them.

Food Uses

Nasturtiums are normally described as "peppery" in taste. My mum and I refer to the plant as the "wasabi plant" both because of the taste that Nasturtiums remind us of, and because we're honestly unable to properly pronounce *Nasturtium*!

Add some leaves to a sandwich or serve egg or chicken salad on a bed of Nasturtium leaves for a zesty meal. Alternatively, stuff the blossoms with cream cheese and serve as an hors d'oeuvre. Nasturtiums can also be cooked with pasta, omelets or used in stir-fries.

Recipe

Nasturtium Stir-fry

Ingredients

1. 1 lb shrimp, peeled and deveined or deboned chicken chunks
2. 2 carrots, peeled and sliced
3. 2-3 c Nasturtium leaves and stems, washed
4. 1 can of baby corn, drained and rinsed or 2 c fresh baby corn
5. 1/2-inch knob of ginger, peeled and minced
6. 2 garlic cloves, peeled and minced
7. 2 Tbsp oyster sauce* or to taste
8. 1 Tbsp soy sauce or to taste
9. 1 Tbsp sesame oil
10. 2 Tbsp Shaoxing cooking wine or dry sherry (optional)
11. 1 Tbsp cornstarch
12. 3/4 c chicken broth or water
13. 2 Tbsp lard or cooking oil
14. Salt to taste.

Method

1. Heat the lard or cooking oil in a wok or frying pan over medium heat.
2. Add the ginger and fry until fragrant but not brown.
3. Add the garlic and stir until softened.
4. Add the carrots and stir occasionally, cooking until softened.

5. Add the shrimp or chicken, stirring until cooked through.
6. Add the baby corn.
7. Add the oyster sauce, soy sauce and stir.
8. In a separate bowl, add the chicken broth or water to the corn starch. Stir until a slurry forms.
9. Add the slurry to the frying pan and mix. Allow the slurry to thicken.
10. Add the cooking wine and mix.
11. Reduce the heat to medium-low and add the Nasturtium leaves.
12. Allow the leaves to wilt before removing the pan from the heat.
13. Add the sesame oil and mix.
14. Salt to taste.
15. Serve hot with steamed rice.

* Available from Asian grocers or Amazon.com

Squash & Nasturtium Butter Pasta

Ingredients
1. 1/2 lb long, thin pasta like linguine
2. 1 1/2 lb baby squash, sliced into thin rounds
3. 18-20 Nasturtium blossoms
4. 1/2 c chicken or vegetable stock
5. 2 tsp fresh thyme
6. 2 tsp fresh parsley
7. 2 shallots
8. 4 Tbsp butter, softened
9. 1 Tbsp salt + salt and pepper to taste

Method
1. Finely chop the shallots, herbs and Nasturtium blossoms.
2. In a bowl, add half the amount of butter and use a fork to mix in the chopped ingredients.
3. Season to taste and set it aside for at least an hour.
4. Add enough pasta cooking water (according to the package directions) and 1 Tbsp salt, to a large stock pot and bring to a boil.
5. Cook the pasta according to the package directions.
6. In a frying pan, melt the remaining butter over medium heat and saute the squash for 2-3 minutes.
7. Add the stock and allow it to simmer while the pasta is cooking.
8. Drain the pasta and toss it with the squash and herbed butter.
9. Season to taste. Serve hot.

- *Recipe by whenharrymetsalad.com*

Stuffed Nasturtium Flowers

Ingredients

1. 8 oz cream cheese, softened
2. 2 Tbsp chives or herb of your choice, minced
3. 12 Nasturtium flowers, picked as close to serving time as possible, cleaned and dry
4. Salt and pepper to taste

Method

1. In a bowl, mix the herbs with the cream cheese.
2. Season to taste.
3. Spoon 1-2 Tbsp (depending on the blossom size) of the mixture into the middle of each flower.
4. Carefully pull the sides of the petals up to cover the cheese as much as possible.
5. Press the petals down lightly into cheese to hold it in place.
6. Serve immediately.

- *Recipe by herbalgardens.com*

Pickled Nasturtium Seeds

Ingredients

1. 2/3 c half-ripened Nasturtium seed pods picked from the vines
2. 1/4 c salt
3. 2 c water
4. 2/3 c distilled white vinegar (5% acidity)
5. 1 tsp sugar
6. 1 bay leaf

Method

1. Separate the seeds from the pods and rise them in clean water to remove any dirt.
2. In a large enough glass container or jar, dissolve the salt in water.
3. Add the Nasturtium seeds into the jar and keep them submerged using a the bottom of another clean glass jar or a glass weight. You can also use a plastic bag to keep the seeds submerged but I try to avoid using plastic when fermenting or pickling.
4. Let the seeds sit at room temperature in the brine for 2 days.
5. Strain the seeds from the brine solution and rinse the seeds with clean water to remove any excess salt.
6. Return the washed seeds into a clean glass jar.
7. In a small saucepan, add the vinegar and sugar and bring to a boil over medium heat.
8. Stir and allow the solution to boil for about a minute.

9. Pour the hot vinegar over the Nasturtium seeds until the vinegar covers them completely.
10. Top with a bay leaf.
11. Allow the jars to cool at room temperature before storing.
12. Cover and store in the fridge or at room temperature.
13. Use in dishes where you might normally use capers.

- *Recipe by gardenbetty.com*

Other Uses

Historically, Nasturtium has also been used for medicinal purposes such as to treat coughs, colds, the flu and menstrual problems. A natural antibiotic, Nasturtiums have also be used topically in poultices for minor cuts and scratches. The leaves have also been rubbed on gums to help to stimulate and clean them.

As a companion plant, Nasturtium is said to repel whiteflies, squash bugs, and striped pumpkin beetles, making it an excellent companion plant to radishes and cabbages. It is also used a trap plant to lure aphids away from other plants. However, I do not have tested the truth of this assertion.

11 SUNFLOWER

Common Sunflower

Most of us know that the striped-hulled Sunflower seeds are edible. Regardless, I think it would be remiss of me to not include this happy-looking, versatile plant in this book. Native to North America, Sunflowers (*Helianthus*) belong to the Asteraceae family. According to Jill MacKenzie of the University of Minnesota, Sunflower were "cultivated for food by native peoples for thousands of years."

This is not surprising -- in addition to its seeds, the flowers, petals, sprouts, leaves and stems are edible. Cultivars like "Arikara", "Mammoth Grey", "Giant White-Seeded", "Tarahumara White Seeded" and "Titan" are mainly bred for their seed production. Additionally, Native tribes also used Sunflowers as a source of medicine, fiber and oil. If you have the room, my suggestion would be to plant a few cultivars for variety.

There are many cultivars of Sunflowers, most of which are tall annual or perennial plants, growing to a height of around a few feet or more. They may bear one or more wide but terminal flower heads that range in color from yellow to orange to red to maroon.

The stem is rough and hairy, with domesticated cultivars usually having unbranched stems and wild varieties having branched stems. They often have sticky petiolate leaves that are dentate, with the lower leaves opposite and often heart-shaped or ovate. The seeds of edible Sunflower seed cultivars are large, compared to the seeds of wild Sunflowers, which tend to be very small.

Cultivation

According to the USDA plant hardiness map, Sunflowers will grow in all US planting zones. Though they are tough plants, they need to be grown in full sun. They will grow in soils of varying acidity (pH 6.0-7.5) as long as the soil is not waterlogged. Once mature, they are drought-tolerant. They are easy to grow and tend to self-sow.

Before planting, be sure to locate your Sunflower planting bed where they will not shade out the surrounding plants when mature. If you are planting tall varieties, plant Sunflowers in an area sheltered from the wind, preferably near something like a fence that you can loosely tie the plant to. Use cloth or a soft material as ties.

While Sunflower seeds are not toxic to humans or animals, they contain a substance that is toxic to grass and may inhibit the growth of some plants. If you do not harvest the heads before the seeds fall out, you'll run the risk of the grass in the surrounding area getting killed. The toxins will eventually biodegrade in the soil but Sunflowers should be planted away from potatoes and pole beans.

If you're planting Sunflowers for their sprouts, you can sow raw, unhulled seeds that have been soaked overnight, closely in a tray filled with potting soil. Cover lightly with more soil and keep it moist but not wet.

Otherwise, to produce mature plants, you can start Sunflowers indoors in individual peat pots up to two weeks before the last frost date. Plant two Sunflower seeds in each peat pot and cover them with a thin layer of soil. Water well and keep the soil moist but not wet. The seedlings should germinate and start growing quickly within a week or two. Transplant after all danger of frost has passed. Thin the weaker seedling out before transplanting.

Unless you have a very short growing season, it is much easier to sow the seeds directly outdoors after all danger of frost has passed. For optimal results, wait until the outdoor soil temperatures have reached between 55-60°F before direct planting.

Before planting, clear the bed of weeds, turn the soil and amend with compost. Space the seeds about 6 inches apart and plant them 1-2 inches deep. If planting in sandy soil, it is better to plant them 2 inches deep. Cover loosely with dirt and keep the area watered until the seeds sprout.

Germination normally takes 7-10 days. Thin the plants to about 2-3 feet apart when the first true leaves appear. Sunflowers will mature in 80-120 days, depending on the variety.

Spread a 2- or 3-inch mulch layer of organic material to help to discourage weeds and to reduce moisture loss from the soil. Once mature, Sunflowers can withstand some drought. However, it's best to keep them regularly and deeply watered, especially during their growing period, which is about 20 days before and after flowering. Regular watering helps root-growth, which is particularly useful if you need to support top-heavy varieties.

If you have poor soil, you may wish to fertilize with a slow-acting fertilizer, which will help to produce larger flowers. Otherwise, Sunflowers do not generally need to be fertilized. Note though, that excessive nitrogen application cause the plant to produce large, green foliage and will delay flowering.

Potential Problems

Deer favor new, tender leaves of the plant tops and can be a problem when it comes to Sunflowers. Garden netting tall enough to keep the deer out, set up around the patch will help to keep the deer at bay.

If you have a large patch, you might have to use a sturdier barrier like electric fencing. In SHTF situations though, your patch might be a good way to lure deer into your yard. The meat from one deer is well worth sacrificing a few Sunflowers for!

Squirrels and birds may become a problem when the seeds ripen and the Sunflowers near harvest time. Cut away the leaves that are closest to the seed heads to make it harder for the critters to perch on. As the seed heads mature, cover each one with cheese cloth which will let air and light in but keep critters out.

There is also a small gray Sunflower moth that lays its eggs on young or developing Sunflower blooms. These moths will create a mass of webbing and debris, feeding on the flower and destroying the seeds. Pick the worms off the plants and kill them.

Sunflowers are fairly problem-free but may suffer from rust and mildew. Mildew looks like a fuzzy mold on the leaf undersides and causes mottling and pale areas especially on the upper leaf surfaces.

It usually infects the older leaves first and will eventually cause the leaves to wither and die. It will not generally kill a mature plant but will mar its appearance. It is usually caused by humidity or contaminated gardening tools so provide the plants with adequate plant spacing, good air circulation and be sure to disinfect your gardening tools before and after use.

Rust usually appears as yellow or white spots, turning brown or black that looks much like rust on upper leaf surfaces. Puffy-looking blisters may later appear on the leaves' undersides. It may also spread to the flowers and stems, distorting the plant's growth. To prevent rust, again provide the plants with good spacing and air circulation. Remove and destroy seriously infected plants as well as all plant debris.

If infected, apply a neem oil spray according to package directions (generally, you'll need to spray a solution of approximately 2 tablespoons of neem oil in 1 gallon of water every 7-10 days until the rust is eradicated).

Disinfect tools by dipping them in a solution of 1 part unscented household bleach to 4 parts water. Keep your hands clean and avoid handling the plants with wet hands.

Harvesting

Harvesting your Sunflowers will depend on the part that you want to harvest. If you're harvesting Sunflower sprouts, which are a tasty treat packed with vitamins and minerals, use a clean, sharp pair of scissors to cut the sprouts off near the base as soon as the first pair of cotyledons (seed-leaves) appear. Rinse the dirt off before use.

Sunflower greens are packed with folate, vitamins, minerals and antioxidants. Harvest young leaves from older plants for use as a cooked green. I would consider Sunflower greens as more of a survival than everyday food.

Remove the tough ribs in the center before cooking. You can remove the bitterness by blanching the leaves with one or more changes of water, much like you would prepare mature dandelion leaves for consumption.

To harvest the flower buds for consumption, pick them off while the flowers are still in the bud stage. Pull the bitter green off the bottom of the bud. The buds can be steamed, boiled or braised and tastes similar to artichokes.

The immature Sunflower stalks can be harvested, peeled and cut into small chunks to be added to salads. The stalks are the part that turn the flowers to face the sun and should still be pliable at the time of harvest.

Avoid harvesting older stalks, which will be tough or woody. Once the flower blooms, you can pluck and harvest the petals. Note though, that it should be used more as an attractive garnish rather than as part of a meal because the petals are bitter.

Finally, the seeds -- normally the part that most people harvest. Check the flower heads in early fall for signs of maturity. The back-side of the flower head should be yellow-brown instead of green (this happens around 30-45 days after blooming), with large flower heads nodding downwards. Within the flower head, you should notice that the tiny petals covering the seeds have dried and are falling out.

It's best to harvest the seed heads before it reaches full maturity, when the birds and squirrels get to them. Collect the seed heads, by cutting the stem off, leaving about a foot or so of the stem attached to the head. Hang the heads upside down in a warm, dry, well-ventilated area and let them cure for several weeks.

If the seeds can be dislodged when you rub two heads together, or when you brush them with your fingers or with a fork, then the seeds are suitably dried.

Otherwise, return the seed heads to their drying position and allow them to dry further. You may also rub the dried flower head against an old washboard for an alternative seed-harvesting method.

Allow the harvested seeds to dry for a few more days in a safe location, away from vermin, before storing them in an airtight container. The seeds are now ready for consumption, sprouting or for propagation.

Propagation

Sunflowers are propagated by seed. Refer the the seed collection and planting procedures in the previous section for the details.

Food Uses

Sunflower seeds are high in proteins, vitamins B and E, minerals (like iron, potassium and phosphorus) and linoleic acid, which helps the body to metabolize fats properly. They can be consumed raw or cooked and used as snacks, as a nut substitute and as a food accompaniment.

The seeds can also be ground into a powder and added to breads, or, much like peanut butter, they can be ground into a Sunflower butter. You can also use the seeds to produce an edible, mildly flavored oil which is suitable for cooking with. When sprouted, the seeds produce delicious, crunchy sprouts that have a bright, almost lemony taste. The sprouts pair well in salads or in sandwiches.

The flower buds or the seed heads can be steamed or braised and served as you would artichokes. The flower petals can be used for garnish or as a tea while the greens can also be used as a tea or be boiled and used as a vegetable. Immature flower stalks once peeled, can work in salads or dishes and the roots can also be used as a tea.

Recipe

Sunflower Seed Flour/Butter

Making Sunflower seed flour is a step towards Sunflower butter. You can use Sunflower flour as an almond flour-substitute. Note that once ground, the oils start to go rancid so be prepared to use your flour or butter within 2-3 weeks of making it. Storing it in the fridge will help to extend its shelf-life.

Ingredients

1. 4 c raw Sunflower seeds, hulled

Add these ingredients to make Sunflower Butter

2. 0-4 Tbsp light-tasting oil of your choice, like avocado oil
3. 1/4 tsp honey (optional)
4. 1/2 tsp salt (or to taste, optional)

Method

1. Preheat the oven to 325°F.
2. On a parchment-lined baking sheet, arrange the hulled Sunflower seeds in a single layer. Avoid overlapping the seeds as much as possible.
3. Bake for about 15 minutes, stirring often until the seeds are golden.
4. Remove from the oven and cool completely.

5. In a food processor, add the Sunflower seeds. Pulse and process. If you have a processor that is smaller than a 14 cup capacity, you will need to process the seeds in separate batches.
6. If you're making Sunflower flour, stop processing once you obtain a flour-like consistency.
7. If you're making Sunflower butter, continue processing until the flour releases the oil and starts to clump.
8. If the seeds are not releasing enough oil, slowly drizzle 1-2 Tbsp of the oil.
9. Continue processing until the oils release more. It should warm up and turn smooth, creamy. Otherwise, slowly add a little more oil until you obtain the desired consistency.
10. Process for another 2-3 minutes.
11. Add the honey and salt to taste and process for half a minute more or until mixed.

Sunflower Bread

Ingredients

1. 1 c boiling water
2. 1/4 c white wheat bulgur
3. 1/2 c Sunflower seeds
4. 1/4 c rolled oats
5. 1 1/2 tsp salt
6. 2 eggs
7. 2 Tbsp vegetable oil
8. 2 Tbsp honey
9. 1 Tbsp granulated sugar
10. 2 tsp instant yeast
11. 3 c + 2 Tbsp unbleached bread flour

Method

1. In a large mixing bowl, add the bulgur and pour the boiling water over it.
2. Allow the mixture to cool until it's lukewarm, about 15 minutes.
3. Add the seeds, oats, salt, eggs, oil, honey, sugar, yeast and enough flour to make a soft dough.
4. On a clean, lightly oiled surface, knead the dough until smooth.
5. Transfer to a lightly greased bowl. Cover and allow the dough to rise for 1-1.5 hours, or until it has doubled in size.
6. Remove the dough from the bowl. Shape it into a loaf, and place it in a lightly greased loaf pan.
7. Using a lightly greased plastic wrap, cover the pan.

8. Allow the loaf to rise until it rises to about 1 inch above the pan's rim, about 45-60 minutes.
9. Remove the plastic wrap and bake the loaf in a preheated 350°F oven for 35 minutes or until a wooden skewer inserted in the middle pulls out clean.
10. If after 20 minutes, the loaf appears to be browning too much, drape a piece of aluminum foil, shiny side up, lightly around the loaf.
11. Once done, remove the pan from the oven and turn the loaf out onto a wire rack. Allow it to cool completely.

- *Recipe by KingAuthorFlour.com*

Stuffed Peppers with Sunflower Seeds

Ingredients

1. 4 bell peppers
2. 1 c rice
3. 1 1/2 c chicken or vegetable broth
4. 1/2 c red onion, peeled and finely chopped
5. 1/4 c black olives, chopped
6. 2 c flat-leaf parsley, chopped
7. 1/2 c finely crumbled feta cheese
8. 1/4 c toasted Sunflower seeds
9. 2 Tbsp balsamic vinegar
10. 1 Tbsp water
11. 1 Tbsp butter, melted
12. 1 tsp dried oregano
13. Salt to taste

Method

1. In a bowl, wash the rice until the water runs clean.
2. In a medium saucepan, add the rice and broth and bring to a boil over medium heat.
3. Cover and lower to a simmer until the rice is cooked and fluffy, about 30 minutes.
4. Preheat oven to 375°F.
5. In a large pot, fill it half full with water and bring to a boil.
6. Cut the tops off the peppers and remove the seeds and the membranes.
7. Immerse the prepared peppers in boiling water.

8. Cover and cook for 4-5 minutes until the peppers are just tender.
9. Coat 4 custard cups or small oven-safe bowls with butter.
10. Stand a pepper upright in each cup.
11. Sprinkle the insides of the pepper with some salt (optional).
12. In a bowl, combine the vinegar, water, butter, salt and oregano and mix well.
13. Add the rice and stir in the onions, olives, parsley, feta and Sunflower seeds.
14. Distribute the stuffing evenly among the peppers, packing it lightly.
15. Place the peppers in the cups on a cake pan and bake in the oven for about 15 minutes or until heated through.
16. Serve hot with any remaining rice-mix on the side.

- *Recipe by sunflowernsa.com*

Sunflower Soup

Ingredients

1. 3 quarts chicken or vegetable stock
2. 2 c Sunflower seeds
3. 1 onion, peeled and chopped
4. 4-5 c fresh spinach leaves, washed and shredded or young Sunflower greens, rib removed and blanched until the bitterness is removed
5. 1/3 c butter or oil
6. 2 tsp savory herb
7. Salt to taste

Method

1. In a pot, heat the oil or butter over medium heat.
2. Add the onions and saute until tender. Do not allow the onions to brown.
3. Add the Sunflower seeds and stock.
4. Cover and simmer for about 40 minutes.
5. Season to taste.
6. Add the spinach or Sunflower greens and savory herbs to the soup.
7. Cover and simmer, about 8 minutes.
8. Pour the soup into a blender or food processor and blend until smooth.
9. Season to taste.
10. Serve hot.

- *Recipe adapted from saturdayeveningpost.com*

Braised Sunflower Heads

Consuming the Sunflower heads will probably be best for larger flower varieties where the seeds are too small to be edible. Otherwise, you will have to choose between having consuming the flower head, or harvesting the seeds later.

Keep the stem on to use as a handle while you prepare the flowerhead. First, pick the petals off (save these for use as a garnish). Trim off the outer edge of the head and remove the green sepals of the calyx (the green petal-looking leaves under the petals). The process should expose the flower head's pith. Turn the flower head over and trim off only the flower's yellow face, leaving the meaty pith.

Now, trim the stem as well as the flower's green underside. The final product should be a large, white, flat heart. You may wish to immerse it in water acidified with a little lemon juice to prevent discoloration from oxidation.

Ingredients

For The Sunflowers
1. 4 large Sunflower heads, prepared as described in the previous section
2. 1 c dry white wine
3. 1/2 c lemon juice
4. 2 fresh bay leaves (or 4 dried bay leaves)
5. 2 basil sprigs, leaves removed & chopped
6. 2 parsley sprigs leaves removed & chopped
7. 2 mint sprigs, leaves removed & chopped
8. 5 thyme sprigs leaves removed & chopped
9. 1/2 c olive oil

10. 1 garlic clove, peeled and thinly sliced
11. sea salt and freshly ground white pepper to taste

Filling

1. 1 c high quality ricotta
2. 1 heaping Tbsp of the chopped herb leaves from the Sunflower braise
3. 1/2 c unseasoned breadcrumbs
4. 2 Tbsp olive oil
5. 1 tsp lemon zest, finely grated
6. 1/2 tsp nutmeg, freshly grated
7. sea salt and freshly ground white pepper to taste

Vinaigrette

1. ~ 1/2 c braising liquid leftover from cooking the Sunflowers
2. 1/2 c olive oil
3. 2 tbsp lemon juice
4. 1 tsp lemon zest, finely grated
5. 1 Tbsp of the chopped herb leaves
6. 1/2 c golden raisins
7. 1/4 c capers, rinsed
8. 2 anchovy fillets, finely minced
9. 1 Tbsp honey
10. White pepper, freshly ground

Method

1. Mix all the vinaigrette ingredients together, and allow it to marinate, undisturbed for at least 30 minutes before using.

2. Place the prepared Sunflowers, face-down in a saucepan.
3. Add the white wine, lemon juice, olive oil, garlic and seasonings.
4. Cover and allow the Sunflowers to braise on low-medium heat for about 45 minutes, or until very tender and lightly browned.
5. Remove the Sunflowers from the pan and allow them to cool.
6. Preheat the oven to 450°F.
7. Place Sunflowers on a baking sheet.
8. In a bowl, mix all the filling ingredients together until well-mixed.
9. Put a large dollop of the filling mixture on each Sunflower, enough to cover each head.
10. Liberally sprinkle the breadcrumbs on each stuffed Sunflower.
11. Bake in the oven for about 7-10 minutes, or until golden brown.
12. Plate the Sunflowers and drizzle the sauce, garnishing with the petals and chopped herbs.

- *Recipe by Charles Draghi (http://hyperurl.co/braisedsunflower)*

Sauteed Sunflower Stems

Preparing Sunflower stems for consumption can be labor intensive so in my view, unless you do not have much else to eat, or unless you have a lot of time to spare, you might want to give the stems a pass.

Harvest the immature stems of the flowers (before they become tough and woody). Peel off the outer layer using a potato peeler. You will lose quite a bit of the edible parts if you use a peeler so, if you have time on your hands and not many stems to peel, you may wish to peel the fibrous layer off using your fingernails. The peeled stem will be about 2/3 - 1/2 its original diameter.

Ingredients

1. 2 c young Sunflower stems, peeled and cut into 1-inch pieces
2. 1 Tbsp Goji berries (Wolfberries), rinsed (optional)
3. 1 Tbsp butter
4. Salt and pepper to taste

Method

1. In frying pan, heat the pan over medium heat.
2. Add the butter and allow it to melt.
3. Add the Sunflower stems and the Goji berries and saute until the stems are cooked but not browned.
4. Season to taste.
5. Remove from the heat.
6. Serve hot.

Other Uses

Oilseed varieties can be dehulled, ground, roasted (at 300°F) and pressed to extract their edible oils. The roasted seed hulls is said to be a usable as a coffee-substitute.

If you have livestock, Sunflower seeds and young greens can also be added to poultry, rabbits and cattle fodder. Consult your livestock veterinarian before changing your livestock's feed.

The dried stems and spent flower heads can be used as litter bedding in hen houses. They can also be used as fire kindling. Sunflower stem fires leave behind an ash that is high in potash that can be used as a garden amendment.

Spread the ash immediately or store covered otherwise, the potash will be washed away if exposed to rain. Use the ash in the amounts of 1/2 to 1 oz of ash per square yard as needed in potato or root crop beds that are being prepared for the following year.

Sunflower fiber can be used in textiles and to make paper. Native Americans also derived dyes from the flower. As a bee plant, Sunflowers help to furnish hives with good amounts of wax and nectar.

Medicinally, its astringent leaves has been used to make a tea used to treat high fevers. When crushed, the leaves are also used to make a poultice (a moist mashup leaf-mass) on sores, swellings or snake or spider bites.

A tea made from the flowers, on the other hand, has been used to treat malaria and lung ailments. The roots have been mashed and boiled in water to make a decoction that is used as a warm wash for rheumatic aches and pains.

12 CONCLUSION

As with earlier books from this series, this book only scratches the surface of the kinds of edible plants you can "hide" in your garden. However, I hope this gives you a starting guide as to the kinds of plants that can work.

Remember that you can also add some of the plants that I covered in "Foraging -- A Beginner's Guide to Edible and Medicinal Wild Plants," like Cattail and Jerusalem Artichokes to your secret edible garden.

Sign up for my newsletter at http://byjillb.com and get THREE books for free:

HOW TO KEEP BACKYARD CHICKENS
CAN DOS & DON'TS
THE MODERN AMERICAN FRUGAL HOUSEWIFE

PLANT-BUYING RESOURCES

Baker Creek Heirloom Seeds (http://rareseeds.com)

Bonnie's Koi and Pond Plants
(http://www.bonniesplants.com/PondPlants.html)

EasytoGrowBulbs.com (http://www.easytogrowbulbs.com/)

Everwilde Farms (http://www.everwilde.com)

Hostas Direct (http://hostasdirect.com)

Johnny's Selected Seeds (http://johnnyseeds.com)

Resortation Seeds (https://www.restorationseeds.com/)

Territorial Seed Company (http://www.territorialseed.com)

The Hosta Farm (http://www.thehostafarm.com/)

Books By Jill b.

Links to books by Jill b. on various platforms can be found at **http://byjillb.com**

The Modern Frugal American Housewife Book #1
Home Economics

The Modern Frugal American Housewife Book #2
Organic Gardening

The Modern Frugal American Housewife Book #3
Moms Edition

The Modern Frugal American Housewife Book #4
Emergency Prepping

How to Keep Backyard Chickens
A Straightforward Beginner's Guide

The Best Backyard Chicken Breeds
A List of Top Birds for Pets, Eggs and Meat

Foraging
A Beginner's Guide to Wild Edible and Medicinal Plants

Medicinal Herb Garden
10 Plants for the Self-Reliant Homestead Prepper

HIDDEN
Prepper's Secret Edible Garden

Can Dos and Don'ts
Water Bath and Pressure Canning

How to Make Money on eBay: Beginner's Guide
From Setting Up Accounts to Selling Like a Pro

How to Make Money on eBay: Maximize Profits
Secrets, Stories, Tips and Hacks - Confessions of a 16-Year eBay Veteran

How to Make Money on eBay: International Sales
Taking the Fear and Guesswork Out of Doing Business Internationally on eBay

Self-Publish on a Budget with Amazon
A Guide for the Author Publishing eBooks on Kindle

About the Author

~ Self-Reliance: One Step at a Time ~
http://byjillb.com

Reliance on one job. Reliance on the agri-industrial food system. Are you ready to break free, take control and to rely on yourself?

With a no-nonsense style, Jill Bong draws from her own homesteading experiences and mistakes, and writes books focusing on maximizing output with minimal input to save you time and money.

Jill writes under the pen name Jill b. She is an author, entrepreneur, homesteader and is the co-inventor and co-founder of Chicken Armor (http://chickenarmor.com), an affordable, low maintenance chicken saddle. She has also written over a dozen books on homesteading and self-reliance.

Jill has been mentioned in various publications including The Associated Press, The New York Times and ABC News. She has written for various magazines including Countryside and Small Stock Journal, Molly Green and Backyard Poultry Magazine. She holds an Engineering degree from an Ivy League from a previous life.

At its height, her previous homestead included over 100 chickens, geese and ducks, as well as cats, a dog, bees and a donkey named Elvis. She currently learning permaculture techniques to apply to her homestead in rural Oregon.

Learn more by visiting her site http://byjillb.com.

References

https://albuquerqueurbanhomestead.com

http://www.almanac.com

http://arcadianabe.blogspot.com

http://bamboogarden.com/care.htm

http://blog.emergencyoutdoors.com

http://blog.kitchenmage.com

http://www.bonniesplants.com

http://botanical.com

http://burpee.com

http://completebamboo.com/bamboo_planting.html

http://eattheweeds.com

http://www.easytogrowbulbs.com

http://espacepourlavie.ca/en/edible-flowers

http://extension.psu.edu

http://garden.org

http://gardeners.com

http://www.gardenersnet.com/flower/lupine.htm

http://www.gardenguides.com

http://www.gardeningknowhow.com

http://www.geeksofgardens.com

http://www.heirloom-organics.com

http://www.herbs2000.com

http://www.hgtvgardens.com

http://homeguides.sfgate.com

https://www.hort.purdue.edu/newcrop/afcm/amaranth.html

https://www.hostasdirect.com

http://www.indianmirror.com

http://www.itmonline.org/arts/bamboo.htm

http://kyotofoodie.com

http://mainehosta.com/hosta_as_a_vegetable

http://mdc.mo.gov/discover-nature/field-guide/american-lotus

http://www.missouribotanicalgarden.org

http://mofga.org

http://motherearthnews.com

North American Native Plant Society (http://www.nanps.org)

http://nature.mdc.mo.gov

http://naturalmedicinalherbs.net

http://mrbrownthumb.blogspot.com

http://www.nhhostas.com/dividing-hostas/

http://www.nola.com/food/index.ssf/2009/09/lotus_seeds_are_known_as_cajun.html

http://onlinelibrary.wiley.com/doi/10.1111/j.1541-4337.2011.00147.x/full

http://olives-n-okra.com

http://www.onlyfoods.net/lupins-lupinus-uses-benefits-nutritional-value-growing-and-care.html

http://www.pfaf.org

http://www.pondplantgirl.com/water-lotus2.htm

https://www.restorationseeds.com

http://www.saga.co.uk

http://www.saltspringseeds.com

https://scottishforestgarden.wordpress.com

http://shesimmers.com/2013/01/lotus-in-thai-cooking-culture.html

https://sproutpeople.org/growing-amaranth-sprouts/

https://www.strictlymedicinalseeds.com

http://superhumancoach.com

http://www.theflowerexpert.com

http://www.thekitchn.com

Swan, D. 2010. *The North American Lotus (Nelumbo lutea Willd.); Sacred food of the Osage People.* Ethnobotany Research and Applications, University of Oklahoma

http://www.tropicalpermaculture.com/amaranth-plant.html

Image Credits

Disclaimer & Disclosure

This book does not contain medical advice. The contents of this book are for educational and informational purposes only. While many plants may have healing properties, the statements and/or uses have not been approved by the FDA. None of the information should be construed as medical advice nor should it be used as a substitute or replacement for conventional medicine, prescription drugs or medical care by a trained medical professional.

Ingesting herbs can interact with medications and interfere with their effectiveness or cause an adverse reaction to occur. Even though there are historical anecdotes of how some herbs have helped with life-threatening conditions, no herbal remedy should be administered without the supervision of a medical professional. Always consult a medical doctor before using any herbal remedies.

This guide is for entertainment and informational purposes only the author and anyone associated with this book shall not be held liable for damages incurred through the use of information provided herein. Content included on this book is not intended to be, nor does it constitute, the giving of financial, legal or professional advice.

The author and others associated with this book make no representation as to the accuracy, completeness or validity of any information in this book. While every caution has been taken to provide the most accurate information, please use your own discretion before making any decisions based solely on the content herein. The author and others associated with this book are not liable for any errors or omissions nor will provide any form of compensation if you suffer an inconvenience, loss or damages of any kind because of, or by making use of, the information contained herein. Any opinion given is the author's own, based on her experience. If in doubt, always seek the advice of a professional who can advise you appropriately before acting on any part of this book.

This book contains references and links to other Third Party products and services. Some of these references have been included for the convenience of the readers and to make the book more complete. They should not be construed as endorsements from, or of any of these Third Parties or their products or services. These links and references may contain products and opinions expressed by their respective owners. The author does not assume liability or responsibility for any Third Party material or opinions.